Ivan Moscovich's
MASTERMIND COLLECTION

Knotty Number Problems
& Other Puzzles

Sterling Publishing Co., Inc.
New York

To Anitta, Hila, and Emilia, with love

Ivan Moscovich Mastermind Collection:
Knotty Number Problems & Other Puzzles was edited, designed, and typeset by
Imagine Puzzles Ltd., London (info@imaginepuzzles.com)

MANAGING EDITOR
David Popey
ART EDITOR
Keith Miller
CONSULTANT EDITOR
David Bodycombe
EDITORIAL ASSISTANT
Rosemary Browne
PUBLISHING DIRECTOR
Hal Robinson

Clipart: Nova Development Corporation

Library of Congress Cataloging-in-Publication Data Available

2 4 6 8 10 9 7 5 3 1

Published by Sterling Publishing Co., Inc.
387 Park Avenue South, New York, NY 10016
© 2005 by Ivan Moscovich
Distributed in Canada by Sterling Publishing
c/o Canadian Manda Group, 165 Dufferin Street,
Toronto, Ontario, Canada M6K 3H6
Distributed in Great Britain by Chrysalis Books Group PLC
The Chrysalis Building, Bramley Road, London W10 6SP, England
Distributed in Australia by Capricorn Link (Australia) Pty. Ltd.
P.O. Box 704, Windsor, NSW 2756, Australia

Sterling ISBN 1-4027-2344-X

For information about custom editions, special sales, premium and corporate purchases, please
contact Sterling Special Sales Department at 800-805-5489 or specialsales@sterlingpub.com

Contents

Introduction

Ever since my high school days I have loved puzzles and mathematical recreational problems. This love developed into a hobby when, by chance, some time in 1956, I encountered the first issue of *Scientific American* with Martin Gardner's mathematical games column. And for the past 50 years or so I have been designing and inventing teaching aids, puzzles, games, toys, and hands-on science museum exhibits.

Recreational mathematics is mathematics with the emphasis on fun, but, of course, this definition is far too general. The popular fun and pedagogic aspects of recreational mathematics overlap considerably, and there is no clear boundary between recreational and "serious" mathematics. You don't have to be a mathematician to enjoy mathematics. It is just another language, the language of creative thinking and problem-solving, which will enrich your life, like it did and still does mine.

Many people seem convinced that it is possible to get along quite nicely without any mathematical knowledge. This is not so: Mathematics is the basis of all knowledge and the bearer of all high culture. It is never too late to start enjoying and learning the basics of math, which will furnish our all-too sluggish brains with solid mental exercise and provide us with a variety of pleasures to which we may be entirely unaccustomed.

In collecting and creating puzzles, I favor those that are more than just fun, preferring instead puzzles that offer opportunities for intellectual satisfaction and learning experiences, as well as provoking curiosity and creative thinking. To stress these criteria, I call my puzzles Thinkthings.

The *Mastermind Collection* series systematically covers a wide range of mathematical ideas, through a great variety of puzzles, games, problems, and much more, from the best classical puzzles taken from the history of mathematics to many entirely original ideas.

This book, *Knotty Number Problems and Other Puzzles,* deals with areas and combinatorial relationships. The Knights of the Round Table provides the challenge to find the right seating arrangements. The famous tangram puzzle, Archimedes' Stomachion is one of the oldest dissection puzzles in existence, among wide variety of different problems.

A great effort has been made to make all the puzzles understandable to everybody, though some of the solutions may be hard work. For this reason, the ideas are presented in a highly esthetic visual form, making it easier to perceive the underlying mathematics.

More than ever before, I hope that these books will convey my enthusiasm for and fascination with mathematics and share these with the reader. They combine fun and entertainment with intellectual challenges, through which a great number of ideas, basic concepts common to art, science, and everyday life, can be enjoyed and understood.

Some of the games included are designed so that they can easily be made and played. The structure of many is such that they will excite the mind, suggest new ideas and insights, and pave the way for new modes of thought and creative expression.

Despite the diversity of topics, there is an underlying continuity in the topics included. Each individual Thinkthing can stand alone (even if it is, in fact, related to many others), so you can dip in at will without the frustration of cross-referencing.

I hope you will enjoy the *Mastermind Collection* series and Thinkthings as much as I have enjoyed creating them for you.

—Ivan Moscovich

How many ways can you solve a problem? Sometimes you need to count. Other situations just require patience. See how you fare with the following puzzles.

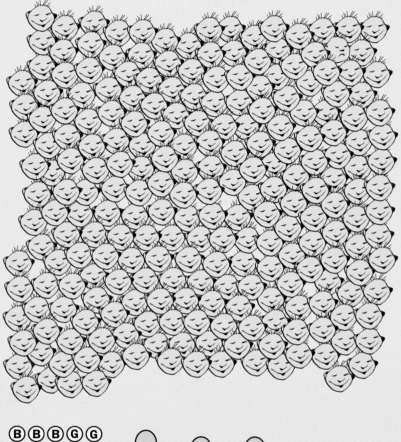

◀ FACE FINDER

How long will it take you to find the sulking face?

ANSWER: PAGE 98

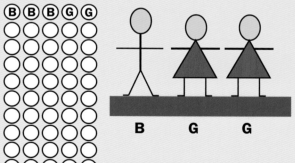

◀ GIRLS AND BOYS IN A ROW

In how many different ways can five children (in any combination of boys and/or girls) be lined up in a row so that every girl is next to at least one other girl?

ANSWER: PAGE 98

▲ TESSELLATION PATTERNS

For each of these patterns, can you tell the minimum number of shapes required to create the floor designs?

ANSWER: PAGE 98

In everyday situations a fundamental order has to prevail. It's how we decide who takes the first turn in a game or what puzzle we should be attempting next.

▲ BOWLING LINEUP

The bowling team has six players. The manager has to choose an ordered lineup of four players.

In how many ways can he do this?

ANSWER: PAGE 98

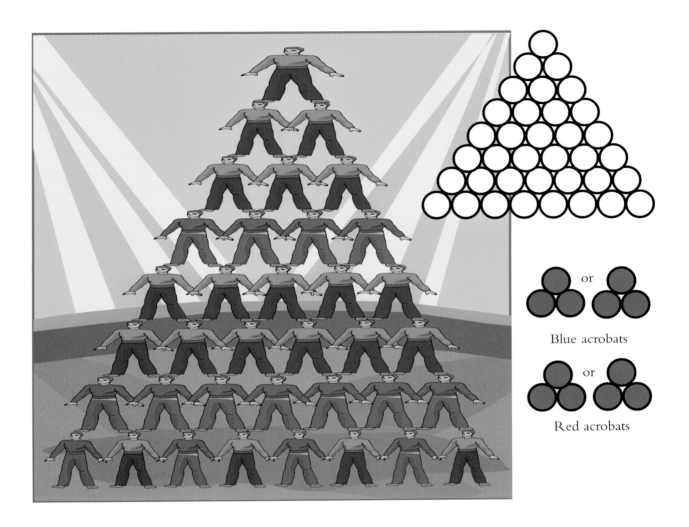

Blue acrobats

Red acrobats

▲ ACROBATS
PUZZLE 1

The human tower created by the 36 acrobats above (21 in blue and 15 in red) requires a lot of strength, planning, and concentration. Also, because of the superstitiousness so common with circus performers, the tower must fulfill the following conditions:

1) *Four red acrobats and four blue acrobats must occupy the lowest row.*
2) *Blue acrobats must stand on one red and one blue acrobat.*
3) *Red acrobats must stand on two red or two blue acrobats.*

   Can you rearrange the tower according to these rules?

PUZZLE 2

Now imagine a much higher human pyramid, in which the bottom row consists of 20 acrobats.

   Without using pencil and paper, can you find a shortcut to determine how many acrobats there are in the whole human pyramid?

ANSWER: PAGE **98**

Finding solutions to pressing problems can lead us to make fascinating discoveries about the world around us. Archimedes probably never imagined that bath time would prove so illuminating.

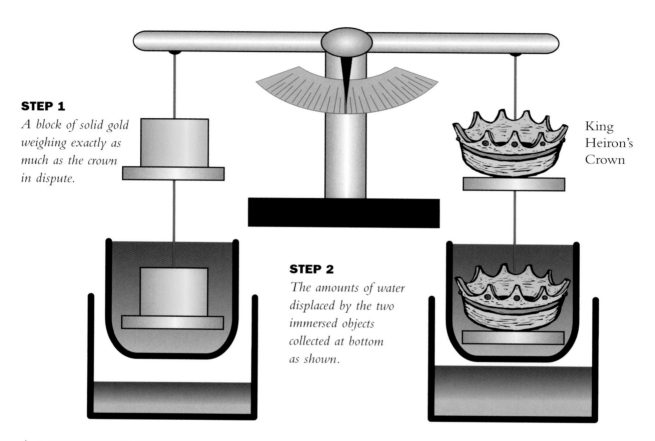

STEP 1

A block of solid gold weighing exactly as much as the crown in dispute.

King Heiron's Crown

STEP 2

The amounts of water displaced by the two immersed objects collected at bottom as shown.

▲ ARCHIMEDES' PRINCIPLE

The Sicilian mathematician Archimedes (ca. 287–212 B.C.), discovering the principle of hydrostatics, so the story goes, ran naked from his bathtub shouting "Eureka" ("I've found it!").

This happened while he was contemplating a problem involving the suspicion that the new crown ordered by King Heiron of Syracuse was not solid gold but also contained other materials. He solved the puzzle without melting down the crown, by discovering the principle today named after him:

One can determine the density of an object (O) by comparing its weight to that of the water it displaces in a bathtub.

The weight of the water, which has the same volume as 'O,' is called O's buoyancy, and the ratio of O's weight to that of the displaced water is called O's "specific gravity."

Step 1: The block of gold is shown to weigh exactly as much as the disputed crown.

Step 2: The same weighing is repeated with both objects immersed in water and the displaced water from both objects is measured as shown.

What was Archimedes' conclusion from this experiment and what is yours?

ANSWER: PAGE **99**

▼ LIQUID BALANCE—BUOYANCY

*Top: The balance is in equilibrium. It carries on one side a container
with water and on the other a stand with a suspended weight as shown.
Bottom: The stand is revolved and the weight is lowered into the
container until it is completely submerged in the water.*

Obviously the pan with the stand becomes lighter.

*The question is, what weight must be added on the pan at right
to restore equilibrium?*

Aɴsᴡᴇʀ: ᴘᴀɢᴇ 99

STEP 1

STEP 2

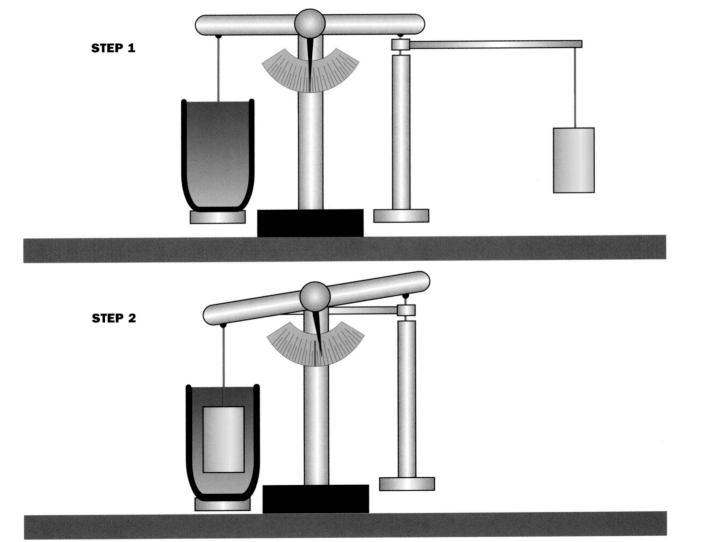

If you used a kaleidoscope as a child, then you'll remember the wonder of mixing the colors to create a beautiful design. But were you ever able to make the same pattern twice? Here's your chance!

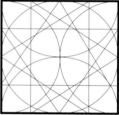

◄ PAIRING PATTERNS

How long will it take you to pair up the 30 tiles on this page with their identical twins on the opposite page?

ANSWER: PAGE 99

All of us use simple mathematics in our everyday lives. For example, we count and list the items we have bought on a shopping trip. But what if we could account for probabilities ahead of time? Read on....

✳ COMBINATORIAL GEOMETRY
Combinations and permutations—counting made easy

One branch of modern mathematics is combinatorics, so named because it studies the ways in which numbers and objects can be combined.

Probability, computer theory, and many everyday situations depend on the principles of combinatorics, specifically on combinations and permutations. The number of possible arrangements in a system may seem small at first, but possibilities rise quickly with the number of elements and soon become impossibly large. The basic instance is simplicity itself:

One object by itself can be arranged in just one way.

Two objects (call them a and b) can be arranged as ab or ba for a total of two permutations.

Three objects—a, b, and c—can be arranged in six ways:

abc,   acb,   bac,   bca,   cab,   cba.

For the general case with n number of objects, the way to work out the permutations is to take the objects one at a time. The first object can fall at any of the n possible positions; for each of those possibilities, the second object can fall at one of n – 1 possible places (since it can't occupy the place the first object takes up); for every one of those n x (n – 1) permutations, the third object can fall in one of n – 2 places; and so on.

In general, for n objects there are n times as many more permutations as there are in systems with only n – 1 objects. For example, there are four times as many possible permutations in a system with four objects than there are in a system with three—in other words, 24 permutations. There are 5 x 24, or 120, different ways to arrange 5 things and 6 x 120, or 720, ways to arrange six things. These numbers are called factorials and are designated with an exclamation point, as in 6!, or six factorial, which equals 720.

Therefore, the general formula for the total number of order, or permutations, of n things is:

$P = n! = n \times (n-1) \times (n-2) \times (n-3) \times ... \times 3 \times 2 \times 1$

This number becomes very large very rapidly.

What about cases that do not deal with ordering one group but finding the permutations of n things taken k at a time? The mathematics here is only a bit trickier. Say you wanted to know how many ordered groups of three can be made from five different elements (such as colors, or letters, or something else).

*"**R**esearch is what I'm doing when I don't know what I'm doing."*
Werner von Braun

✳ Combinatorial geometry continued

You would calculate:

$$_nP_k = \frac{n!}{(n-k)!} = \frac{5!}{(5-3)!} = \frac{5 \times 4 \times 3 \times 2 \times 1}{2 \times 1} = \frac{120}{2} = 60$$

Sometimes we are not concerned about the order of the things (permutations), but are only interested in the combinations we can make from the sample in question. A combination is a set of things chosen from a given group where no significance is attached to the order of the things within the set.

The general formula for the total number of combinations is:

$$_nC_k = \frac{n!}{k!(n-k)!} = \frac{5!}{3!(5-3)!} = \frac{5 \times 4 \times 3 \times 2 \times 1}{(3 \times 2 \times 1) \times (2 \times 1)} = \frac{120}{12} = 10$$

Up to this point we have been dealing with objects which are all different. Sometimes it may be the case that there are a number of identical things of differnet sorts, such as sugar cookies (a), ginger snaps (b), Oreos (c), etc. In this case the number of permutations is determined by this formula:

$$P_{a,b,c} = \frac{n!}{a!b!c!}$$

Most probabilities relating to games and puzzles can be determined by counting the total number of possibilities and the number of outcomes having some desired property. The ratio of these two numbers gives the probability. The formulas for permutations and combinations facilitate and shorten the counting. The values for the number of combinations of n elements taken k at a time can be obtained from the well-known Pascal's triangle.

Combinatorial problems have attracted mathematicians since antiquity. Magic squares were mentioned in the I Ching, a Chinese book dated to the 12th century B.C. Pascal's triangle (not using that name) was taught in 13th-century Persia.

In the West, combinatorics began in the 17th century with Blaise Pascal and Pierre de Fermat in connection with their development of the theory of probability, and later with the work of Gottfried Wilhelm Leibniz. Leonhard Euler was responsible for the development of combinatorial mathematics in the 18th century. He became the father of graph theory when he solved the Königsberg bridge problem.

Many combinatorial problems were presented in the 19th century as recreational problems (the problem of eight queens, the Kirkman school girl problems). Among the earliest books on combinatorics is Percy MacMahon's *Combinatory Analysis* (1915).

Choices, choices everywhere! Whether it's a night out at your local restaurant or your ambitions of winning big in the lottery, you're going to have to do a bit of brainwork before coming those crucial decisions.

MENU

CHICKEN SOUP
VEGETABLE SOUP

WHOLE CHICKEN
FRIED PORK
STEAK

BLACK FOREST TORTE
ICE CREAM

▲ **THREE-COURSE MENU**

How many different three-course meals can you choose?

ANSWER: PAGE 99

▼ LOTTO

In a popular lotto game, a player must choose six different numbers between 1 and 54. The order of the numbers is not important.

In how many different ways can a player make his or her choice?

ANSWER: PAGE 99

It's comforting to know that even King Arthur may have had problems seating his knights around the famous round table in different combinations each time. Think yourself lucky when there's just six people to arrange.

▲ ROUND TABLE

What is the number of different possible ways to seat three married couples, alternating males and females, around a table, with the three husbands placed so that none of them sits next to his wife?

ANSWER: PAGE 100

▲ KNIGHTS OF THE ROUND TABLE

There are 21 different ways eight knights can be seated around the round table so that no one has the same two neighbors more than once.

One arrangement is shown, with the knights numbered from 1 to 8.

This is not an easy combinatorial problem. Your task is to try to find as many of the 21 different arrangements as you can.

ANSWER: PAGE 100

Arranging things just the way you like them can be quite a task. Sometimes serendipity intervenes and things work the first time but often you just have to sit down and puzzle it out.

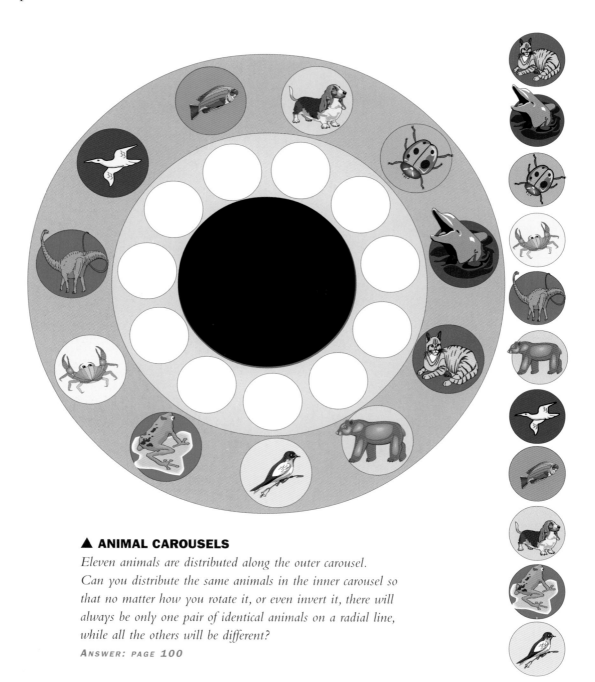

▲ ANIMAL CAROUSELS

Eleven animals are distributed along the outer carousel. Can you distribute the same animals in the inner carousel so that no matter how you rotate it, or even invert it, there will always be only one pair of identical animals on a radial line, while all the others will be different?

ANSWER: PAGE **100**

◀ ICE CREAM CONES

You order a triple-scoop cone made with strawberry, vanilla, and melon ice cream. What is the probability that the scoops will be arranged in the order you like to eat them, from the top to the bottom?

ANSWER: PAGE *100*

Aprinciple is a standard rule that describes a fundamental law or the behavior of a system. See if you can work out the principles behind the following problems.

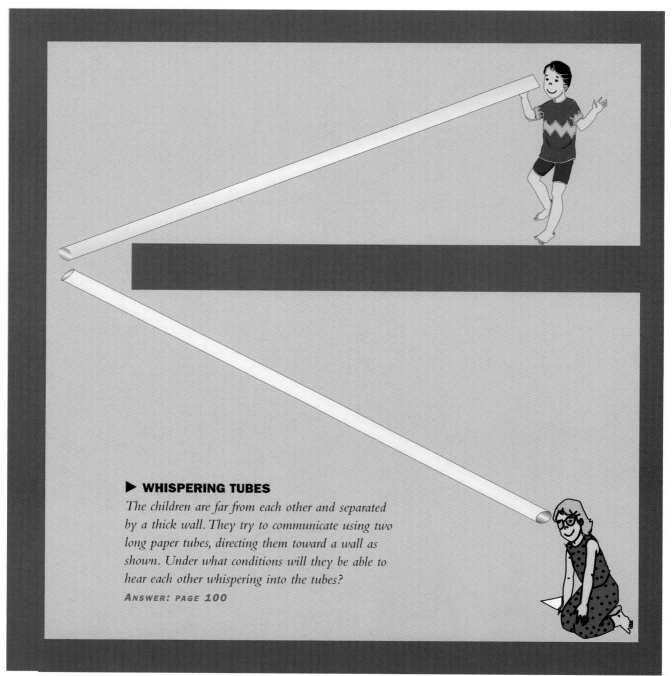

▶ WHISPERING TUBES

The children are far from each other and separated by a thick wall. They try to communicate using two long paper tubes, directing them toward a wall as shown. Under what conditions will they be able to hear each other whispering into the tubes?

ANSWER: PAGE **100**

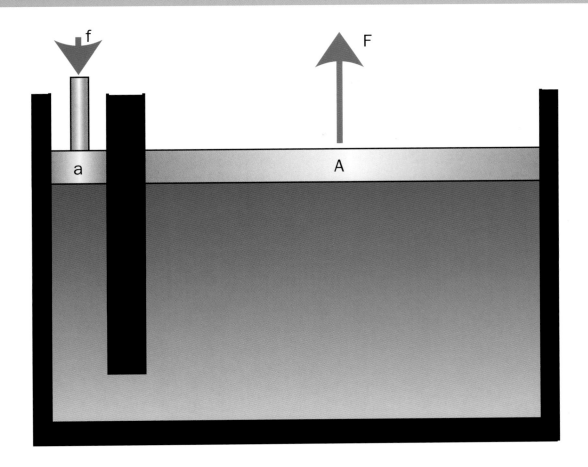

$$\frac{f}{a} = \frac{F}{A}$$

$$\text{or } F = \frac{f \times A}{a}$$

▲ PASCAL'S PRINCIPLE

The demonstration model shows the operation principle of a hydraulic press and enables one to figure out its mechanical advantage. It consists of two cylinders, with a piston in each cylinder.

When a fluid is placed in a closed container, any change in pressure at one point in the fluid is transmitted undiminished to all points of the fluid. This conclusion was reached over 300 years ago by the French philosopher Blaise Pascal. All devices used to pump liquids from one place to another take advantage of this principle.

Devices like hydraulic lifts, presses, and jacks, as well as the hydraulic brake system, exemplify Pascal's principle.

The dimensions of the model are:
Area of the small cylinder: 3 cm²
Area of the large cylinder: 21 cm²
The mechanical advantage is 21 ÷ 3 = 7

Can you work out how much force should be applied to the small piston to lift the big piston a distance of one unit?

ANSWER: PAGE 101

We see regular polygons everyday—in street signs, on wallpaper patterns, or on tiled floors. Now take a look around and see how many complicated polygon formations you can see—there are more than you think.

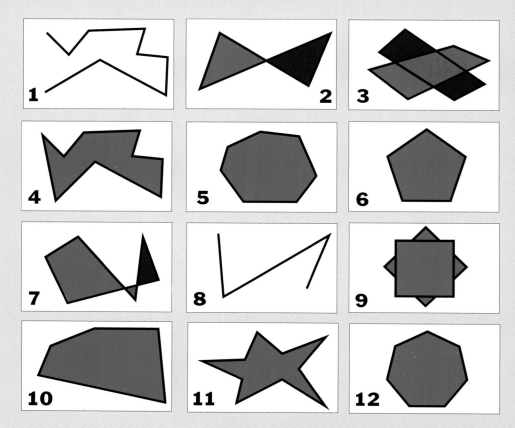

▲ POLYGONS AND LINES

A polygon is called regular if it has the following two properties:

1) All its sides are equal.

2) All its angles are equal.

A circle may be thought of as a regular polygon of an infinite number of sides.

An open polygon is one in which the last side does not end where the first side begins.

A closed polygon is one in which the last side ends where the first side begins.

A simple polygon is a closed polygon in which no two sides cross one another. A simple polygon divides the plane into two parts, an interior and an exterior.

A complex polygon is one in which the sides intersect, dividing the polygon into more than two parts.

A compound polygon is one composed of more than one superimposed polygon.

A convex polygon can be identified by taking any two points inside the shape; if the straight line between those two points always lies inside the shape, the polygon is convex.

Can you work out which polygons are regular, open, closed, simple, complex, compound, convex, and non-convex?

ANSWER: PAGE 101

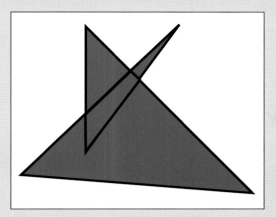

◄ CROSSED POLYGONS

This is a closed crossed polygon of five edges.

Note: One or more of the puzzles below may be impossible.

Puzzle 1 *Can you draw a closed polygon of six edges, such that every edge intersects exactly one other edge (at a point other than a corner point)?*

Puzzle 2 *As before, but so that every edge intersects exactly two other edges?*

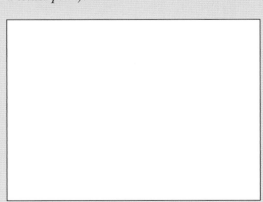

Puzzle 3 *Can you draw a closed polygon of seven edges, such that every edge intersects exactly one other edge?*

Puzzle 4 *As before, but so that every edge intersects exactly two other edges?*

ANSWERS: PAGE 101

Acircle can be thought of as a polygon with an infinite number of sides. The combination of two or more circles can create fascinating polygonal results.

▼ CHORD INTERSECTIONS

Three sets of three intersecting circles are shown.
    Can you find the intersection points of their common chords, join these points and tell what polygon will be the result?

ANSWER: PAGE 101

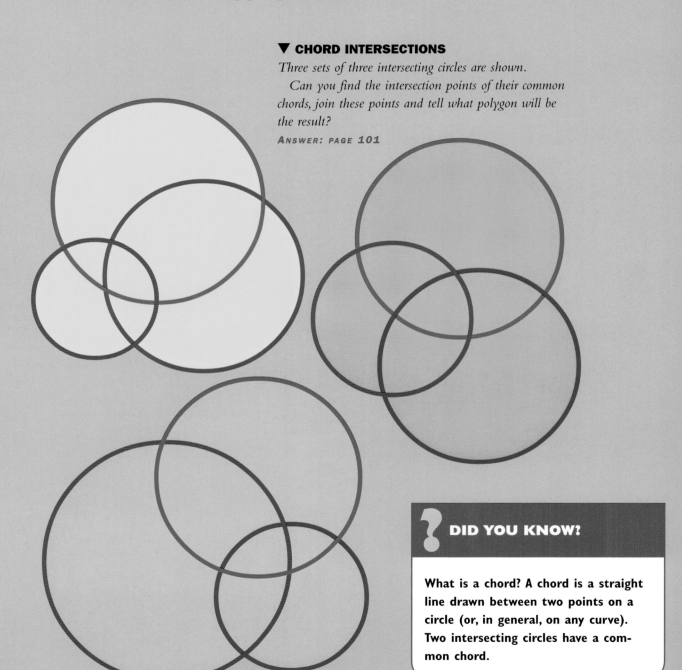

❓ DID YOU KNOW?

What is a chord? A chord is a straight line drawn between two points on a circle (or, in general, on any curve). Two intersecting circles have a common chord.

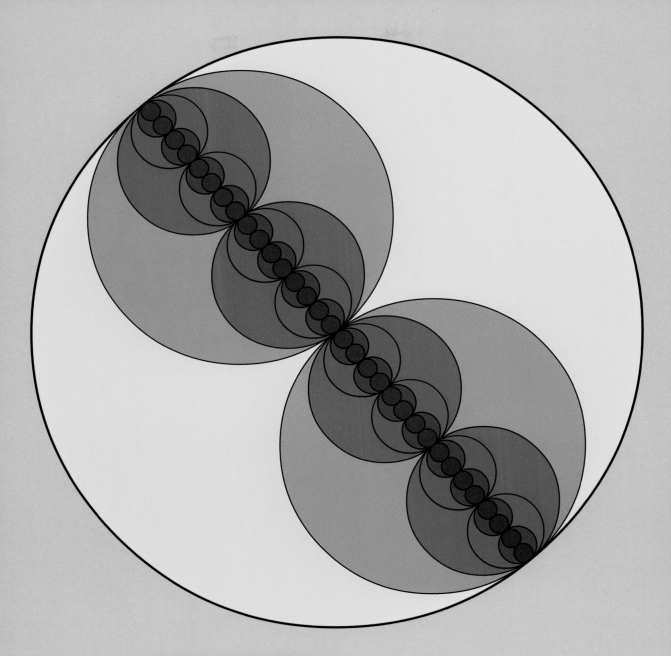

▲ TO INFINITY WITH CIRCLES

The progression of circles inside the circle goes on to infinity.

Can you work out the relationships between the full area of the big yellow circle of one unit radius and the full areas of the five colored sets shown within?

ANSWER: PAGE 102

Imagination is a key element in the mind of the mathematician. Without creative foresight we might not have had some of the greatest inventions—or the perplexing puzzles—that you will find in this book.

◄ SEE THROUGH

Imagine that each of these tiling patterns has been printed on a piece of clear film (with the white tiles being clear). In your mind's eye, can you reconstruct the pattern you would see if all three pieces of film were placed exactly on top each other?

ANSWER: PAGE 102

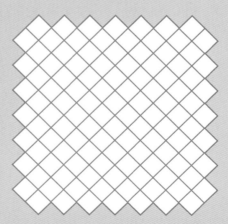

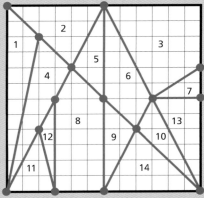

1	2	3	4	5	6	7	8	9	10	11	12	13	14

▲ ARCHIMEDES' STOMACHION

This beautiful dissection puzzle, similar to tangrams and attributed to Archimedes (according to a 10th-century Greek manuscript) is called Stomachion, or "Archimedes' box."

The puzzle consists of 14 pieces forming a 12-by-12 square. As with the tangram, the object of the game is to rearrange the pieces to form abstract and figurative figures or patterns.

In the Greek manuscript the areas of the Stomachion pieces are defined. Can you work out the areas of the 14 pieces of Stomachion?

You can copy and cut out the 14 colored pieces (above, left) to make figures.

At above right is the structure of the puzzle with its lattice points on a 12-by-12 square grid.

ANSWER: PAGE *102*

Stars, like any other shape, can be either regular or irregular. All the stars in the night sky may be irregular in shape and size, even though we prefer to think of them as regular, shining objects of perfection.

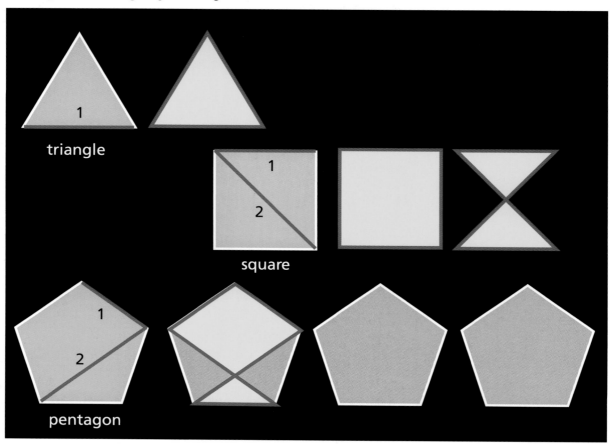

▲ POLYGON-STAR TRANSFORMATIONS 1

The rules of transformations demonstrating the relationships of irregular star patterns to their regular polygons are as follows:

From any point of a polygon a continuous line is drawn, touching all points of the polygon once before returning to the original point, so as to create a symmetrical pattern, as demonstrated by the diagrams above.

The lines allowed to be used to create the stars are shown in red. The triangle is unique and has no different transformations; for other polygons there are different possible

transformations to create star patterns. For example, the square has two different transformations, while with other polygons there is a rapid increase in the number of possible transformations.

Revolutions and mirror-image reflections of the patterns are not considered different.

How many different possible symmetrical transformations can you find for the regular pentagon?

Hint: There are three different symmetrical irregular pentagonal stars, one shown. Can you find the others?

ANSWER: PAGE 102

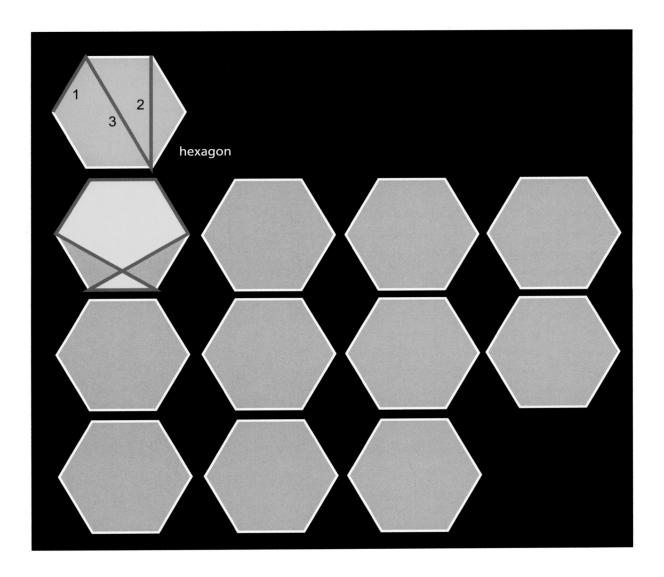

hexagon

▲ POLYGON-STAR TRANSFORMATIONS 2

*According to the rules given on page 30, how many
different possible transformations can you find for the regular
hexagon?*

*Hint: There are eleven different symmetrical irregular
hexagonal stars, one shown. Can you find the others?*

ANSWER: PAGE 103

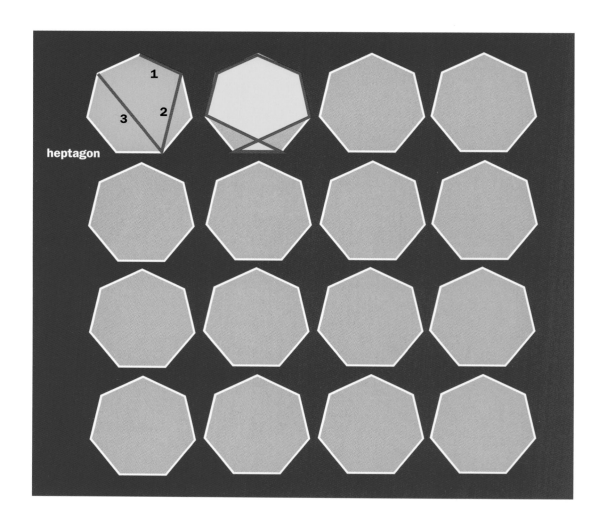

▲ POLYGON-STAR TRANSFORMATIONS 3

According to the rules given on page 30, how many different possible transformations can you find that can be applied to the regular heptagon?

Hint: There are 23 different symmetrical irregular heptagonal stars, one shown. Can you find at least 14 others?

Answer: page 103

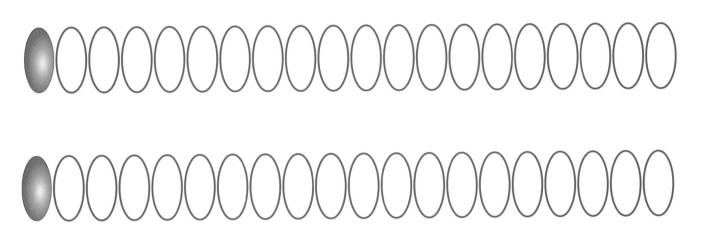

▲ TWO-COLOR BEAD STRINGS

You have a supply of ten beads each of two colors, red and blue, arranged in a string starting with a red bead.

Let us call any group of consecutive beads in a string a "word." The length of a word is the number of beads in it.

A word of length 2 is a couplet. How many couplets are possible?

A word of length 3 is a triplet. How many triplets are possible?

A word of length 4 is a quadruplet; length 5, a quintuplet; and so forth. In general, a word of length 'n' is called an n-tuplet.

How long can a two-color string be if no couplet in it appears more than once?

How long can a two-color string be that has no duplicated triplets?

ANSWER: PAGE 104

It's not commonly known, but both stars and rainbows have their own mathematical logic. The way in which a rainbow appears to the human eye relies on the geometry of reflection. The distance of stars can be calculated by the length of time it takes their light to reach us here on earth.

▲ STAR HEXAGONS

Six points are equally distributed along the circumference of a circle. The six points are interconnected in different possible ways by a closed line forming irregular hexagonal stars, a selection of which is shown above.

Can you find the odd one out?

ANSWER: PAGE 104

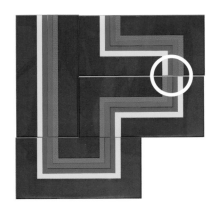

The circled area is joined incorrectly.

▲ RAINBOW LOOP

Copy and cut out the 18 2-by-1 rectangles above.

The object of the puzzle is to put the rectangles together in a 6-by-6 square configuration to form a continuous closed loop of four colors.

ANSWER: PAGE 104

A machine that replicates patterns might be used to produce clothes or carpets. Having a sweater with a puzzle on it means you would never be lost for something to do!

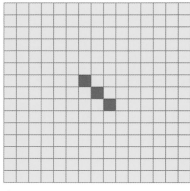

1

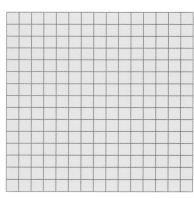

2

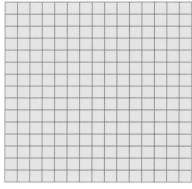

3

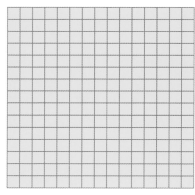

4

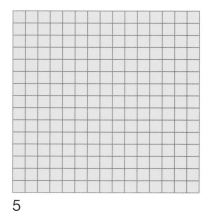

5

◄ FREDKIN'S AUTOMATON

Fredkin's cellular automaton was one of the earliest self-replicating machines. The pattern to replicate is shown in its initial position. Each successive grid holds a new generation of cells that have been added or subtracted according to a simple rule:

If the number of red cells horizontally or vertically adjacent to the cell is even, then the cell is yellow in the next generation; if the number of adjacent red cells is odd, the cell is red in the next generation (this rule is depicted visually in the inset below).

How many generations will be needed until the pattern is replicated?

ANSWER: PAGE 105

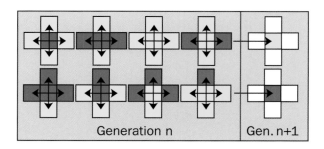

Generation n   Gen. n+1

▲ OVERHAND KNOT

The overhand knot is the simplest knot, having only three crossings, as shown above right. It is also known as the thumb knot and forms the basis of many other knots.

In our puzzle the lower end of an overhand knot passes twice more through the loop as shown. Will the knot disappear when the ends of the rope are pulled?

ANSWER: PAGE *105*

▲ MINIMAL NEIGHBORHOOD

My friends live in ten buildings along the same long street as shown. I would like to find a house in the street at a spot that minimizes the sum of all distances from my friends.

Where should this spot be?

ANSWER: PAGE 106

✳ Plateau's problem

Soap films can be employed for beautiful demonstrations of some of the laws of calculus, as they almost instantly stretch across wire frames to form the one single minimal surface that connects the wire cages and has the least possible amount of surface area. Once the existence of a solution has been demonstrated by a physical model, it may then be possible to complete the extremely complex mathematical analysis of what is known as Plateau's problem—to find the surface of the smallest area bounded by the given contour in space.

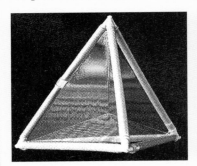

Minimal surfaces in a skeleton of a tetrahedron and cube.

◄ SOAP RINGS

A wire structure is formed by two parallel circular rings joined along the same axis as shown.

Can you guess what the shape of the minimal surface formed will be when the structure is dipped into a soap solution?

ANSWER: PAGE 106

Favoring one hand over the other can be decribed as a result of social conditioning rather than an innate ability. For example, if you couldn't use your preferred hand, over time you might find that the other would function perfectly well.

▲ LEFT- AND RIGHT-HANDED

The children in the classroom are either left-handed, right-handed, or ambidextrous. For this puzzle, we will consider ambidextrous children to be both left-handed and right-handed.

One seventh of the left-handed are also right-handed, and one ninth of the right-handed are also left-handed.

Are more than half of the children right-handed?

ANSWER: PAGE **106**

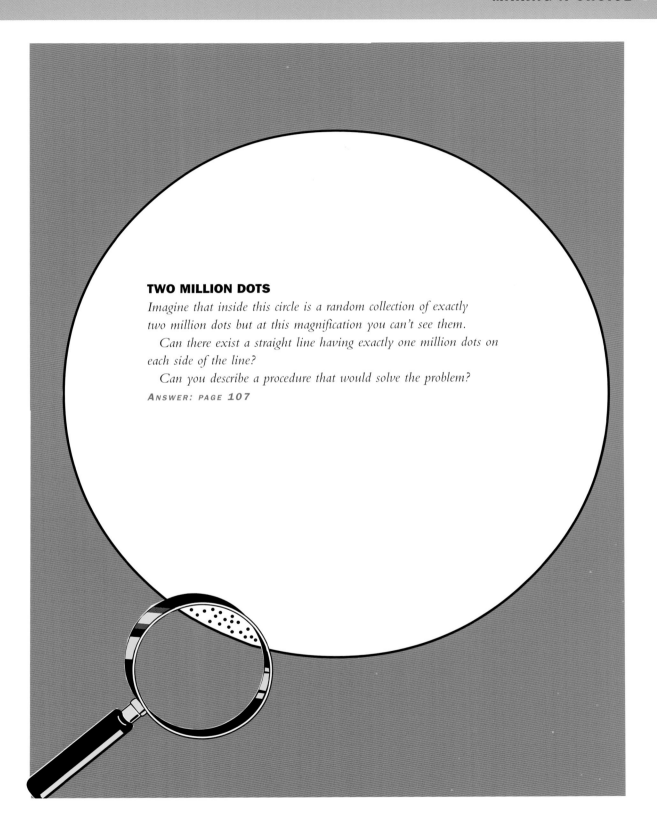

TWO MILLION DOTS

Imagine that inside this circle is a random collection of exactly two million dots but at this magnification you can't see them.

Can there exist a straight line having exactly one million dots on each side of the line?

Can you describe a procedure that would solve the problem?

ANSWER: PAGE *107*

Concentration is a key skill in completing complicated mathematical problems. One interruption and you can find that all your work is forgotten. A simple solution? Write everything down!

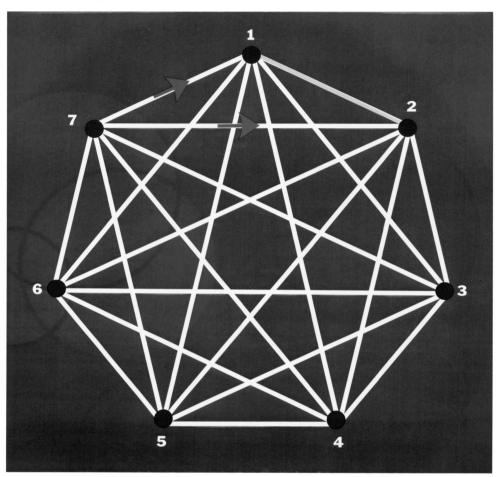

▲ DIGRAPH ARROW TRIANGLES

If an arrow is added to each line of a graph, giving each line a direction, the graph becomes a directed graph, or digraph.

A complete graph is a graph in which every pair of points is connected by a line. (A complete graph with seven points is shown above.) By assigning a direction to each line of a complete graph, one makes a complete digraph.

The object of this puzzle is to transform the above graph into a complete digraph by adding an arrow to every line, so that for any two points it is always possible to get to each point in one step from some third point. An example is provided for points 1 and 2 in the graph, showing that from point 7, only one step is needed to get to either of them.

Can you add the rest of the arrows to fulfill this condition for all points?

ANSWER: PAGE 108

► **CHESSCUBE**

How many cubes of any size are there in a 3-D chesscube?

ANSWER: PAGE *108*

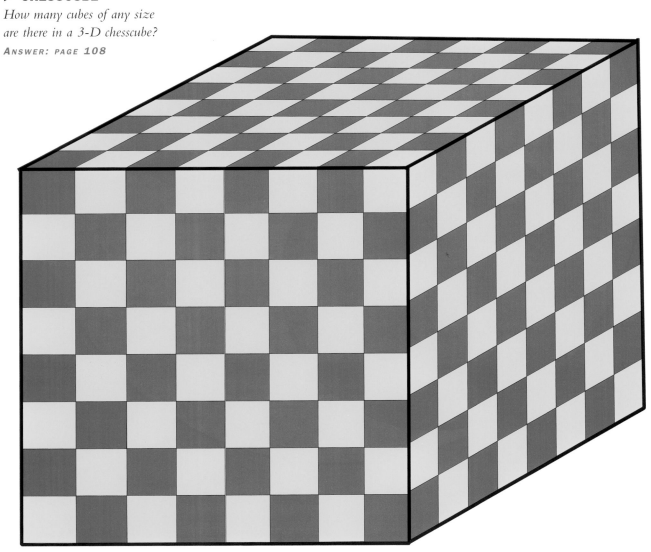

Standard jigsaws are easy because we can very quickly see the relationship between the elements in the picture. The following puzzles work in the same way but are, of course, much more difficult.

▶ RED-BLUE-GREEN RING

Can you work out the relationships between the combined red, blue, and green areas in the circular ring? Note: the larger circle is twice the radius of the smaller circle.

ANSWER: PAGE 108

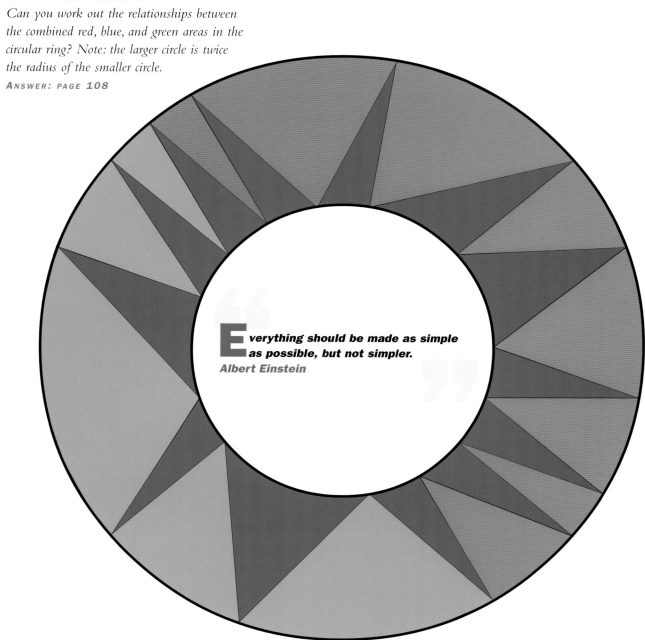

"Everything should be made as simple as possible, but not simpler."
Albert Einstein

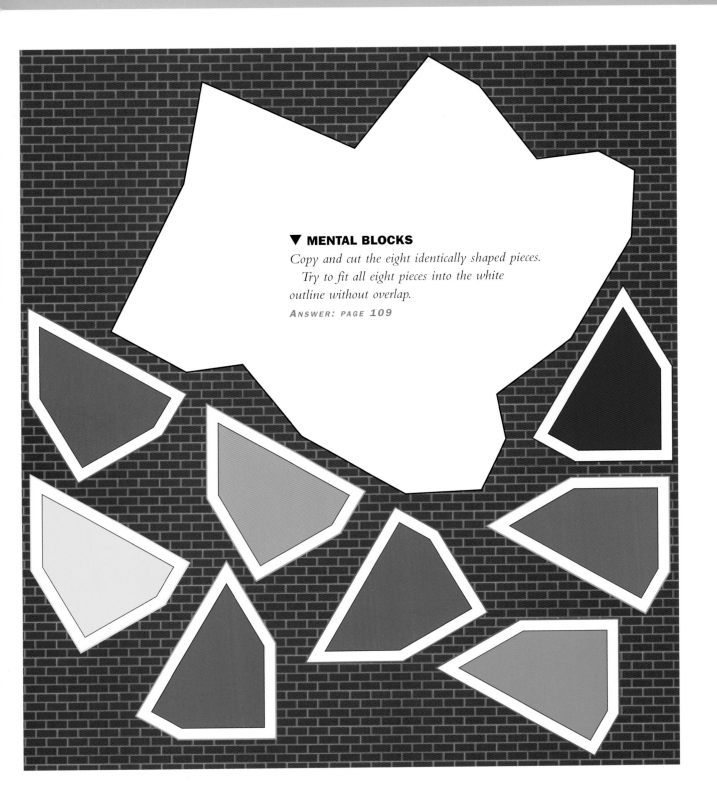

▼ **MENTAL BLOCKS**

Copy and cut the eight identically shaped pieces.
Try to fit all eight pieces into the white
outline without overlap.

ANSWER: PAGE *109*

The next move or the right shape to choose in a game is sometimes glaringly obvious—but what is it that makes us choose so quickly? Experience? Intuition? Think about how you make the correct decisions on these pages.

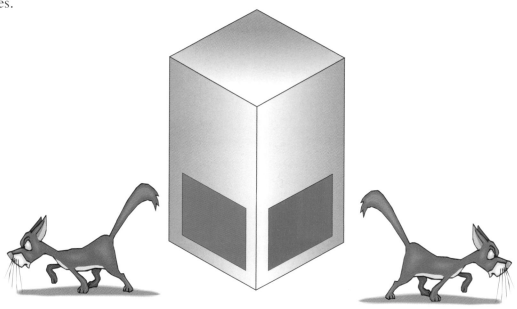

▲ CAT IN A FLAP

Look for a moment at the drawing of the cat doors above, cover it, then look at the bottom drawings and try to choose the right red and blue doors.

ANSWER: PAGE 109

▼ **CONNECTION**

Can you draw lines to connect pairs of identical colors along the white gridlines? Lines may not cross.

ANSWER: PAGE 109

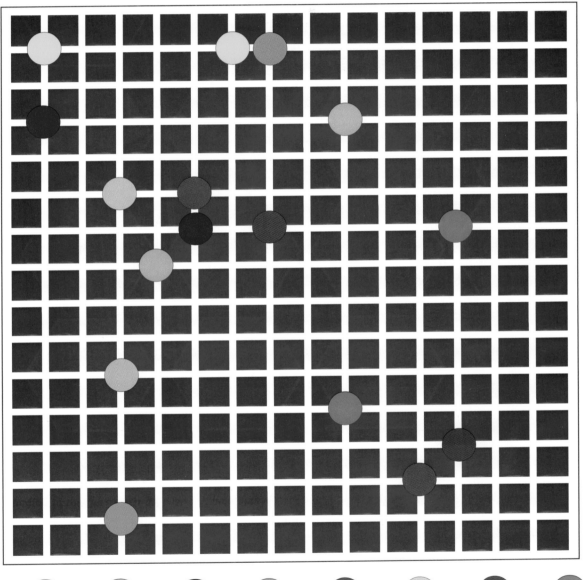

Combination—the word instantly conjures up an image of a secret password, but it could easily apply to an efficient arrangement of resources. Read on to try different ways of ordering things—numbers and people!

▲ PASSWORD

The bank account password of the gentleman opening his account consists of three letters followed by two digits:

How many passwords are possible:
Puzzle 1) When any letters and digits are allowed?
Puzzle 2) When no repetition of letters and digits is allowed?
Puzzle 3) As in Puzzle 2, but the password must start with a "T"?

Answer: page 109

18.4

▲ CAMOUFLAGE

Eight soldiers are hidden in the forest so that none of them can see each other. Each one is located on a white circle in the grid and through their nightscopes they can see only along the straight grid lines, horizontally, vertically, and diagonally.

Can you place the eight soldiers accordingly?

ANSWER: PAGE 109

Pegboards are a good way to understand the area relationships between different shapes. As the boards get bigger there are more twists and turns required to produce each shape than you may first imagine.

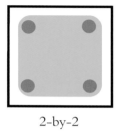

2-by-2

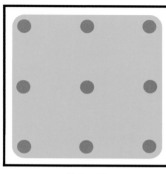

3-by-3

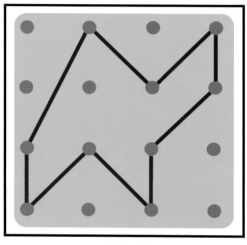

4-by-4

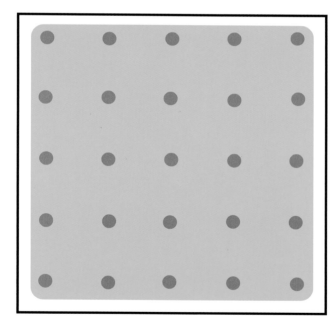

5-by-5

◀ PEGBOARD CLOSED POLYGONS 1

Pegboards are useful learning aids for understanding polygons and area relationships— and solving puzzles.

Closed polygons whose edges are not continuous (that is, an edge must make a turn after reaching a peg) are drawn on square pegboards of different sizes.

Corners of the polygons must be on the pegs of the boards and no peg can be used more than once.

On a 4-by-4 pegboard a closed polygon has been drawn with 9 corners.

Can you draw such a polygon with corners on all 16 pegs?

In general, what is the maximum number of pegs on which such polygons can be drawn for 2-by-2 to 5-by-5 squares?

ANSWER: PAGE 110

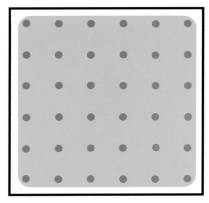

6-by-6

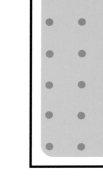

7-by-7

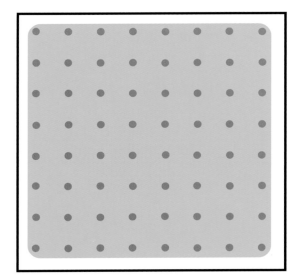

8-by-8

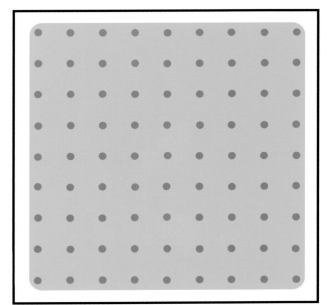

9-by-9

▲ PEGBOARD CLOSED POLYGONS 2

Following the rules on page 50, can you draw polygons on these pegboards (6-by-6 to 9-by-9), using every peg on each board?

ANSWER: PAGE 110

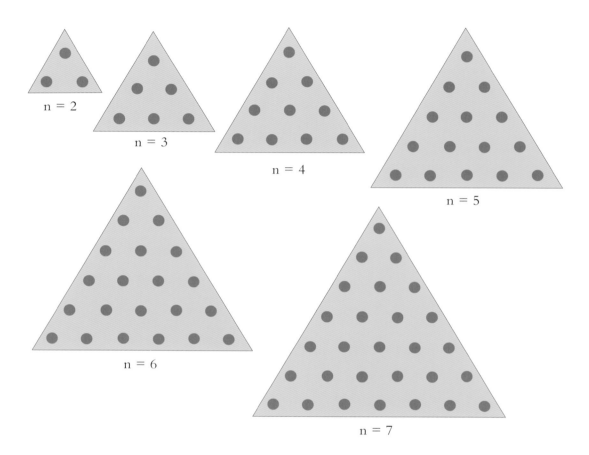

n = 2

n = 3

n = 4

n = 5

n = 6

n = 7

▶ PEGBOARD CLOSED POLYGONS 3

Following the rules on page 50, what is the maximum number of pegs that can be occupied by drawing closed polygons on each of these triangular pegboards?

ANSWER: PAGE 111

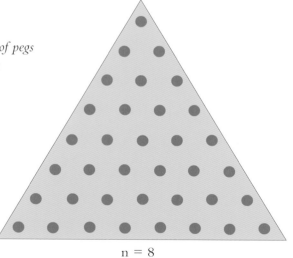

n = 8

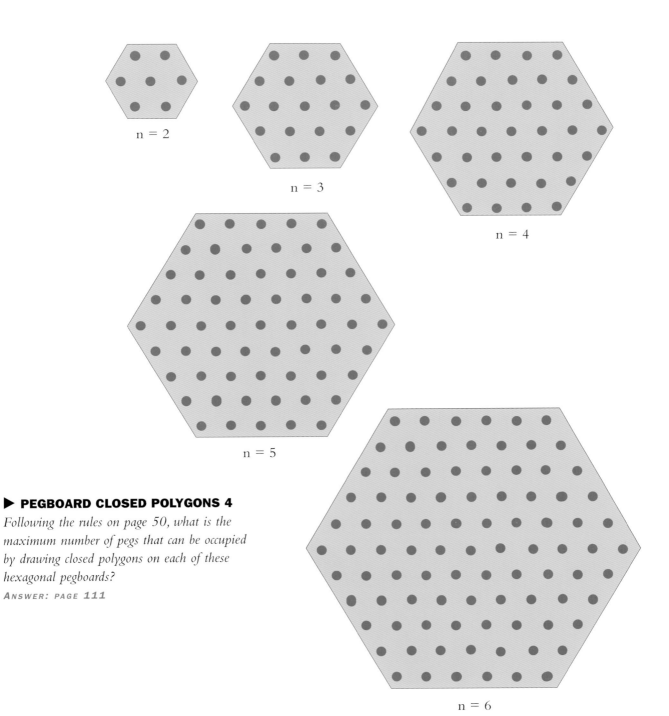

n = 2

n = 3

n = 4

n = 5

n = 6

▶ **PEGBOARD CLOSED POLYGONS 4**

Following the rules on page 50, what is the maximum number of pegs that can be occupied by drawing closed polygons on each of these hexagonal pegboards?

ANSWER: PAGE 111

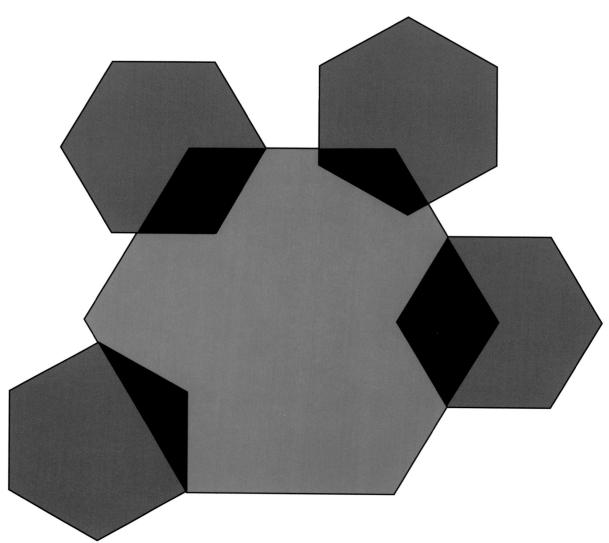

▲ OVERLAPPING HEXAGONS

Four small hexagons are overlapping the large hexagon, as shown.

Which area is bigger: the sum of the green areas of the small hexagons or the red area of the non-overlapping part of the large hexagon?

The sides of the large hexagon are twice as long as the sides of the small hexagons.

ANSWER: PAGE *112*

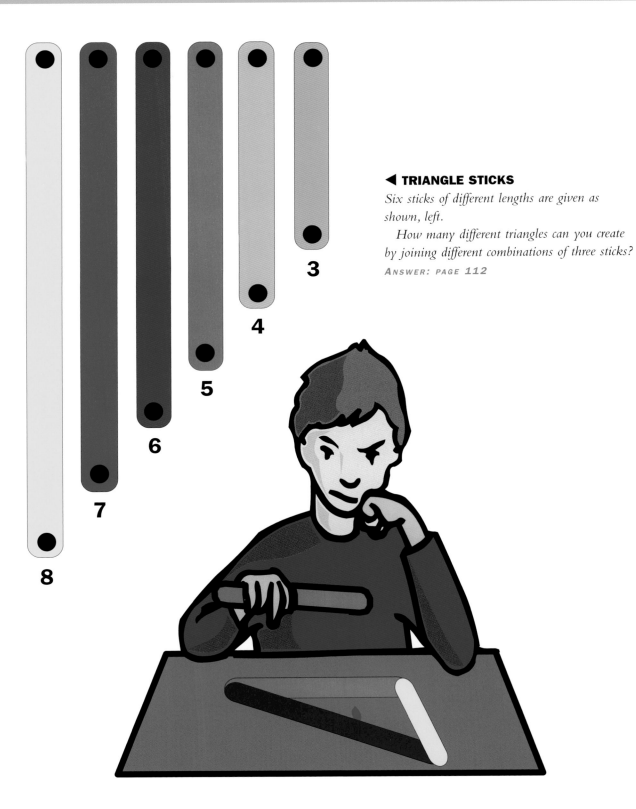

◄ TRIANGLE STICKS

Six sticks of different lengths are given as shown, left.

How many different triangles can you create by joining different combinations of three sticks?

ANSWER: PAGE *112*

3

4

5

6

7

8

▼ **CONNEXT**

Can you connect the 18 consecutive points with a closed non-intersecting line?

ANSWER: PAGE 112

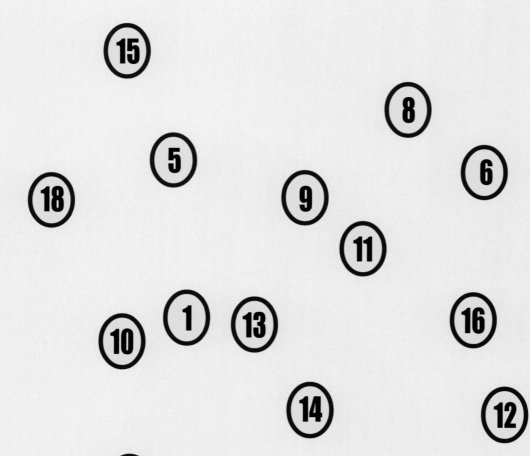

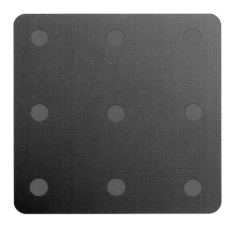

◄ PEGBOARD QUADRILATERALS

PUZZLE 1 *How many different quadrilaterals can you draw by connecting pegs on a 3-by-3 pegboard?*
Can you draw 16 without intersecting sides?

PUZZLE 2 *In how many different ways can you divide the 3-by-3 pegboard into four shapes with equal areas? The areas do not need to be congruent.*

Can you find 10 different ways? Reflections and rotations are not counted as different.

ANSWER: PAGE 113

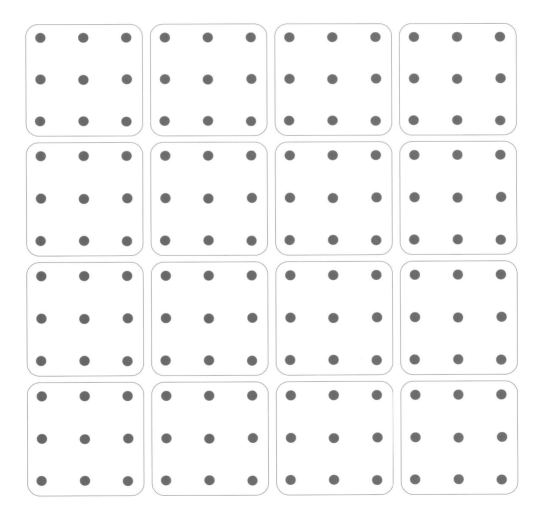

W e're often fooled by first glances. What at first appears simple may soon become one of the trickas you proceed on the following pages.

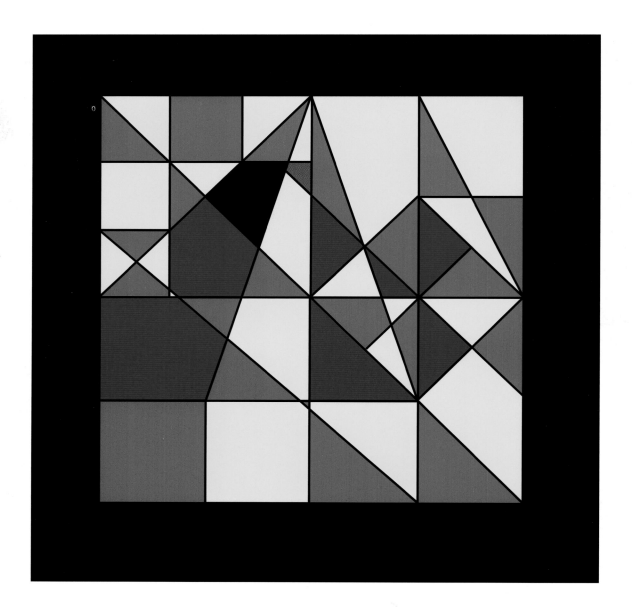

▲ HOW MANY SQUARES 1?

How many squares of any size are there in the pattern?

ANSWER: PAGE 114

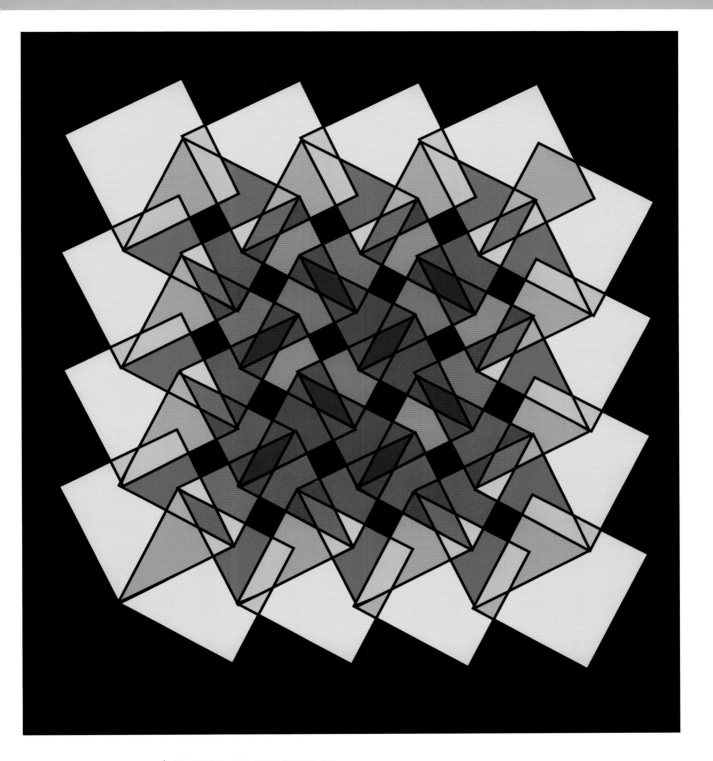

▲ HOW MANY SQUARES 2?

ANSWER: PAGE 114

The thought we give to delineating an area really depends on the subject matter. We may think little about providing equal space for every part of a garden but pay lots of attention to cutting equal slices of a cake.

❈ Area perimeter: The island problem

When lines on a piece of paper define space, they define area—which is two-dimensional space. But even paper has depth, and so the flat piece of paper is really a surface. Beneath a surface is a volume—which is three-dimensional space.

As any primary schoolteacher knows, area and perimeter are difficult ideas to grasp.

Children are not the only ones who are confused by area, volume, and perimeter. Clever packaging of products fools many adults into thinking that they are buying more than they really are. Areas and volumes are easy to estimate for rectangular shapes and boxes; estimating is more difficult for other shapes, especially ones with curved sides.

The ancient Greeks knew the significance of perimeter in terms of area enclosed—indeed, the word meter is derived from the Greek word for "measure around." Since many Greeks lived on islands, they had good reason to be aware of the pitfalls of measurement. After all, it is easy to see that the area of an island cannot be assessed using the time it takes to walk around it; a long coastline might simply mean that the shape of the island is irregular rather than meaning that the island is large. Nevertheless, the custom was for landowners to base real estate on the perimeter of their holdings, not the area.

An example of how this problem has been circumvented is in the ancient story of Dido. As a princess of Tyre, she fled to a spot on the North African coast. There she was given a grant of land that was terribly small—equal to what could be covered by the hide of an ox. Undaunted, Dido had the hide cut into strips and sewn together to make one ribbon about a mile in length. Then, using the shoreline as one boundary, she had her supporters stretch the ribbon of hide in as big a semicircle as was possible. In this way one ordinary ox hide encompassed about 25 acres of land. On that spot Dido founded the famous and powerful city of Carthage.

Her solution to her quandary was based on the fact that of all the plane figures with the same perimeter, the circle always has the largest area. Today this is called the "isoperimetric theorem."

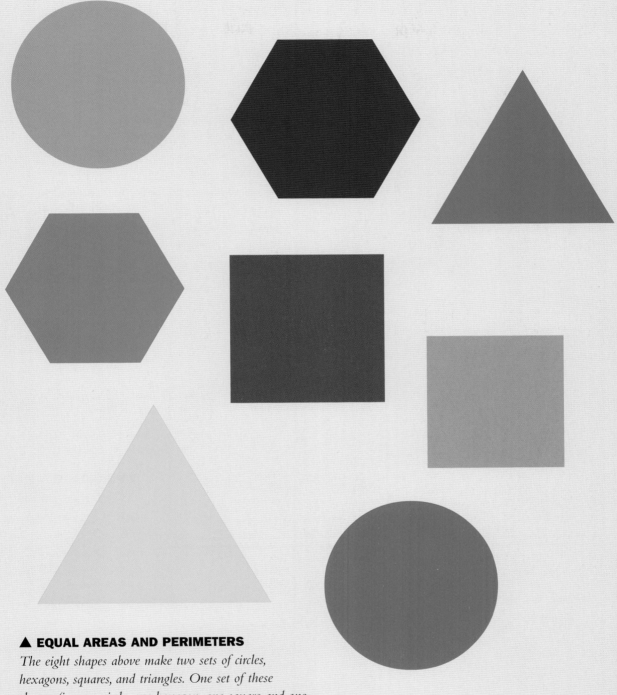

▲ EQUAL AREAS AND PERIMETERS

The eight shapes above make two sets of circles,
hexagons, squares, and triangles. One set of these
shapes (i.e. one circle, one hexagon, one square and one
triangle) all have the same areas; the other set of four
all have the same perimeters.

Can you sort out the two sets, those with equal areas
and equal perimeters?

ANSWER: PAGE 114

When trying to calculate the size of an area on a pegboard try looking for shapes within shapes. Even the oddest forms can become simple to work out when you take this approach.

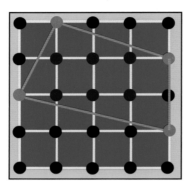

◀ PEGBOARD SHAPES 1

The pegboard on the left has a rubber band stretched around four red pegs, enclosing an area.

Can you determine this area, in terms of unit grid squares, without actually measuring anything?

ANSWER: PAGE 114

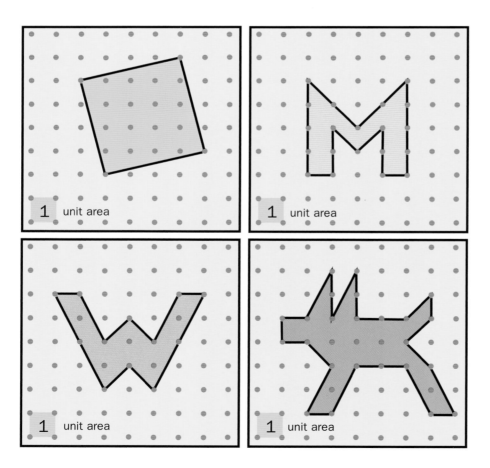

◀ PEGBOARD SHAPES 2

Just by looking, can you tell the areas of the four shapes on the pegboards, in terms of the unit square area illustrated?

ANSWER: PAGE 115

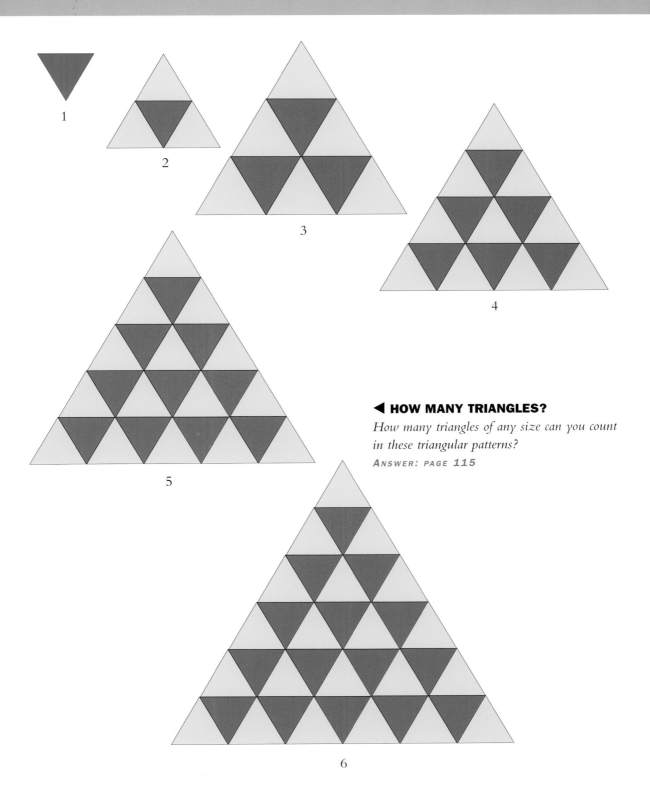

◄ HOW MANY TRIANGLES?

*How many triangles of any size can you count
in these triangular patterns?*

ANSWER: PAGE 115

Pegboards can be used as practical methods of solving problems of area, arrangement, and angle. One wonders why we don't play with them more often!

▼ PEGGING SQUARES

The white circles represent pegs on a pegboard. You have 16 rubber bands in different colors with which to form squares. The object of the puzzle is to place the 16 rubber bands around the pegs according to the following rule:

Each peg can be only a corner of one square, but it can be part of an edge of another square, as shown by the two sample rubber bands placed in the pegboard.

ANSWER: PAGE 115

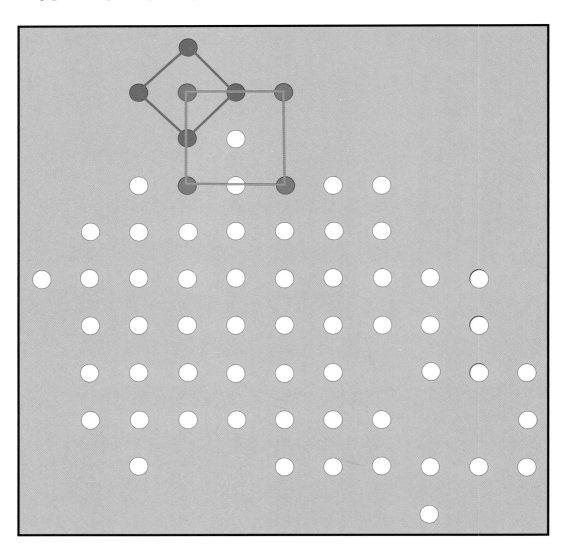

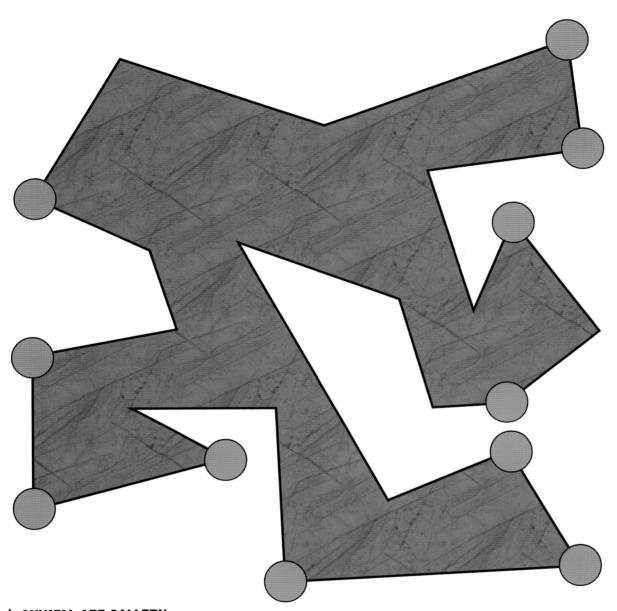

▲ CHVATAL ART GALLERY

In this strangely shaped art gallery consisting of 24 walls, revolving security cameras can be mounted at any corner. In the example shown, 11 cameras (red dots) have been installed.

However, the cameras are expensive to install and maintain. What is the minimum number of cameras required so that every square inch of the gallery is covered by at least one camera?

ANSWER: PAGE 116

Mathematicians have the ability to see generalizations and hence familiar solutions crop up again and again for seemingly very different problems—much like a boomerang, in fact.

▼ ANGLES IN A TRIANGLE

By folding paper, how can you prove that the sum of the three angles in a triangle equals 180 degrees on the Euclidean plane?

Can there be other surfaces on which the sum of the angles in a triangle is smaller or larger than 180 degrees? I can think of several such triangles that exist in the real world.

ANSWER: PAGE 116

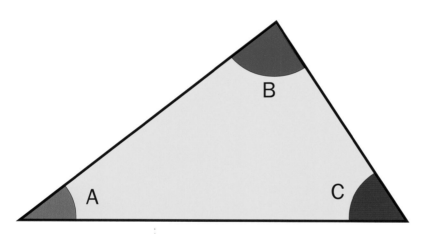

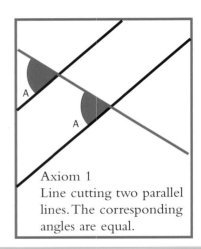

Axiom 1
Line cutting two parallel lines. The corresponding angles are equal.

❈ Proving the angles in a triangle

There are a few things that might worry you about the above puzzle: that the results may have worked only for this specific triangle, or that small unnoticable gaps have been created in the folds, or that folding the paper changed the angles somewhat. You can, of course, reduce your worries by trying the same folding proof with different triangles, but still you may never know whether a triangle may exist that will not produce the same results.

The first lesson about mathematical thinking and problem solving is that we have to think in generalizations and not in specifics, providing a mathematical proof. Such proofs could be found only after ancient Greek mathematicians made geometry abstract. They idealized points and lines, creating an abstract world to which the laws of geometry they created could apply with perfect accuracy. They also knew how to obtain practical results from their idealizations, making geometry deductive based on axioms.

The process of Euclidean geometry was first discussed in Euclid's book *Elements*, which was for centuries the ultimate textbook of human reasoning. To use this process to obtain mathematical proofs to problems we have to get acquainted with "axioms"—for which no proofs are given nor are necessary—used as starting points in search of "theorems." The power of the axiomatic method is this: If you believe the axioms, you have to believe the theorems too. But should we believe in axioms? The ancient Greek geometers would have answered that you "just see" the truths of axioms.

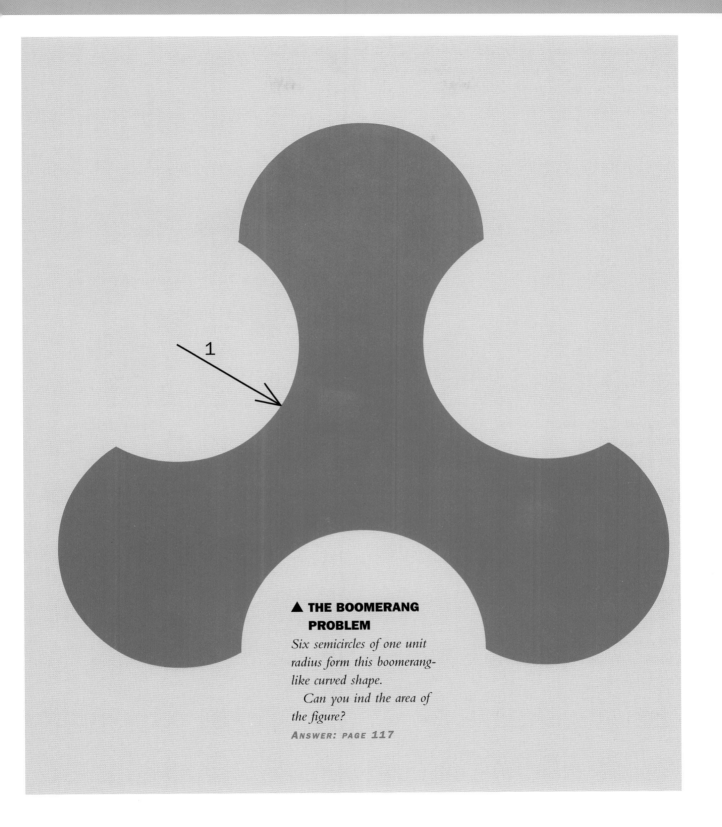

1

▲ THE BOOMERANG PROBLEM

Six semicircles of one unit radius form this boomerang-like curved shape.

Can you ind the area of the figure?

ANSWER: PAGE 117

A little knowledge goes a long way. As you manipulate the shapes on these pages think about how they combine to create new mathematical spaces—how can these be defined?

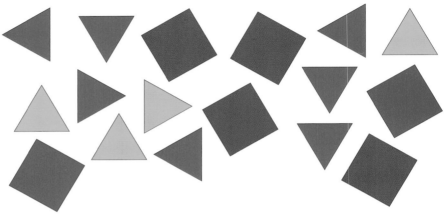

▶ JOINING SQUARES AND TRIANGLES

You have a supply of equilateral triangles and squares with identical sides.

We can see at right the number of triangles and squares needed to create convex polygons with up to 10 sides.

How many triangles and squares will be needed to create the smallest convex polygon of 11 sides?

ANSWER: PAGE 117

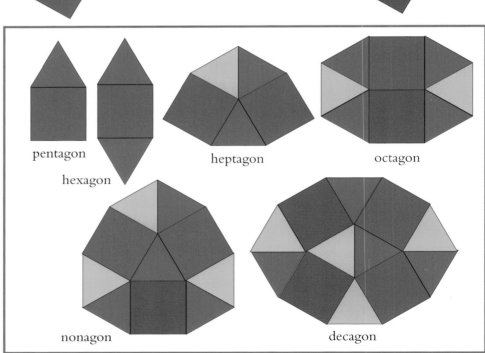

pentagon

hexagon

heptagon

octagon

nonagon

decagon

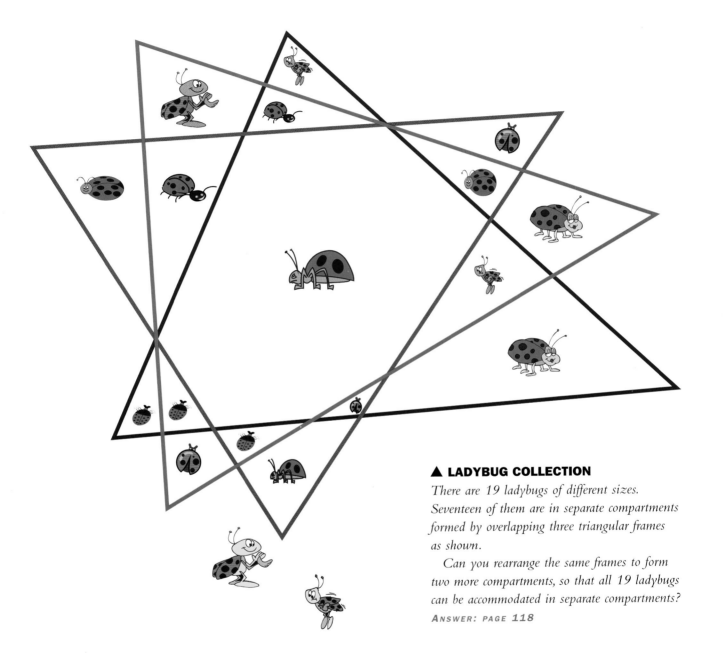

▲ LADYBUG COLLECTION

There are 19 ladybugs of different sizes. Seventeen of them are in separate compartments formed by overlapping three triangular frames as shown.

Can you rearrange the same frames to form two more compartments, so that all 19 ladybugs can be accommodated in separate compartments?

ANSWER: PAGE 118

Getting from A to B (and, for that matter, C and D) in the least amount of time is a problem we face every day. Teleportation is an obvious solution but that's far in the future. For now, let's think about the puzzles on these pages!

❊ Minimum Steiner Trees

If you have a certain number of points randomly scattered in the plane, an obvious problem that arises is how they can be interconnected by straight lines having the minimum possible total length.

In such problems we can distinguish between minimum spanning trees and minimum Steiner trees (which are minimized by adding one or more extra points, or Steiner points). Both are demonstrated below for three and four points.

Jakob Steiner, a Swiss geometer (1796–1863) was the first to investigate minimal problems.

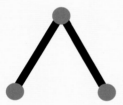

Length 2

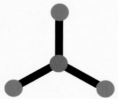

Length 1.74

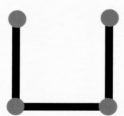

Length 3

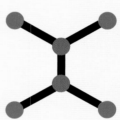

Length 2.73

THREE POINTS
Minimum spanning tree for three points of an equilateral triangle.

THREE POINTS
Minimum Steiner tree for three points of an equilateral triangle. By adding an extra point the length is minimized.

FOUR POINTS
Minimum spanning tree for the four points of a square.

FOUR POINTS
Minimum Steiner tree for the four points of a square. By adding two Steiner points the length is minimized (one extra point won't work here).

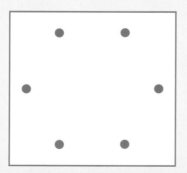

◀ **SHORTEST ROUTES IN A HEXAGON**

What is the minimal road network for connecting the six points of a regular hexagon?

Can you provide answers for both a minimum spanning tree and a minimum Steiner tree?

ANSWER: PAGE 119

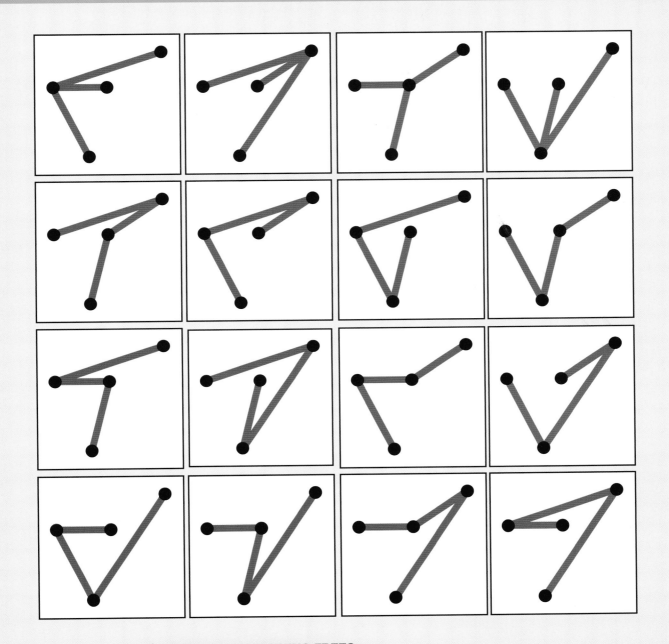

▲ FOUR-TOWN SPANNING TREES

Four towns are situated as shown.

There are 16 possible different spanning trees interconnecting the four towns with straight lines. The towns are represented by dots and roads by lines.

Which is the shortest among them?

ANSWER: PAGE 119

Often as much pleasure can be derived from manipulating a puzzle in your mind as actually solving it—especially when the answer is well hidden.

▲ **THE TURN PUZZLE**

Can you discover the secret rule of the turn and reveal the name of the puzzle?

ANSWER: PAGE 119

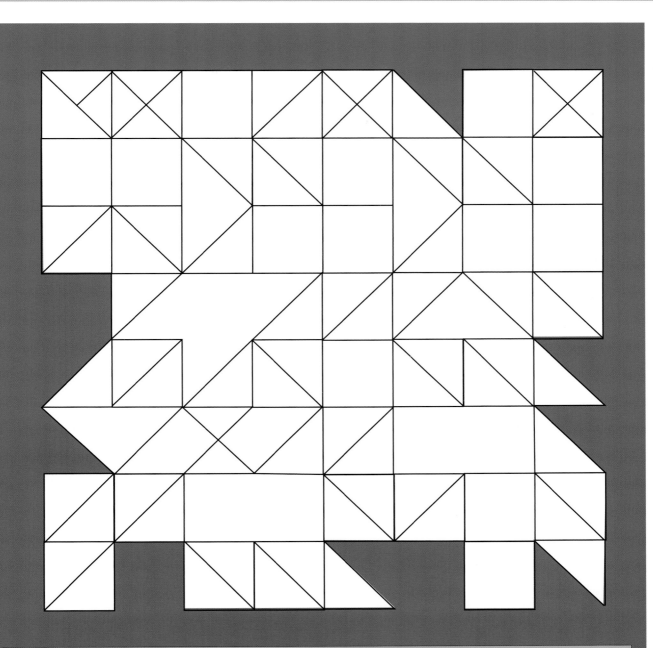

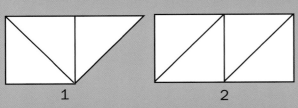

1 2

◀ HIDDEN OUTLINES

How many times can you find the two outlines at left in the pattern above?

They must appear in the pattern above in exactly the same orientation as shown at left. Other lines may cross them.

ANSWER: PAGE 119

When a cake is divided equally it's easy to give out portions. But how do you decide who gets what when someone has been less than accurate with the knife? Time for a little mediation, perhaps?

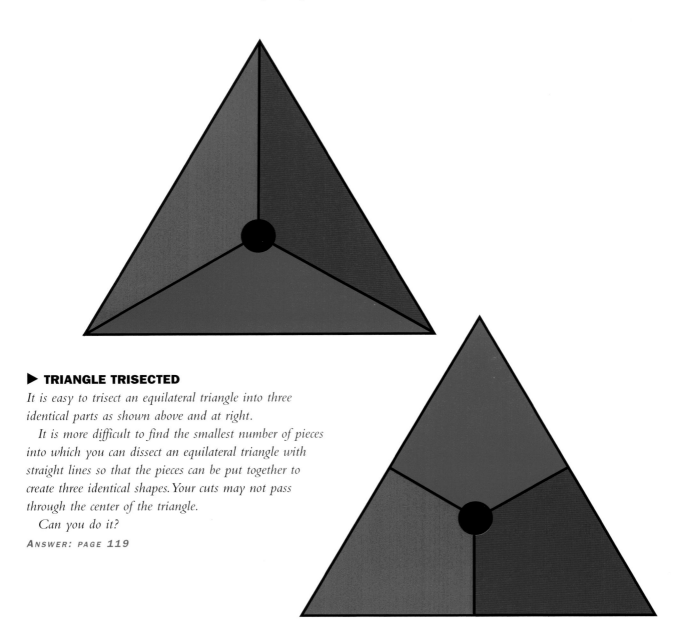

▶ TRIANGLE TRISECTED

It is easy to trisect an equilateral triangle into three identical parts as shown above and at right.

It is more difficult to find the smallest number of pieces into which you can dissect an equilateral triangle with straight lines so that the pieces can be put together to create three identical shapes. Your cuts may not pass through the center of the triangle.

Can you do it?

ANSWER: PAGE **119**

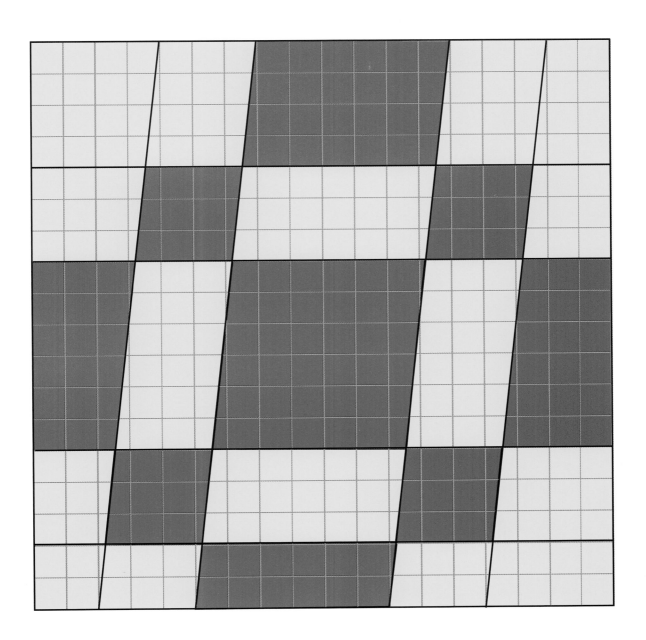

▲ **SQUARE GRID**

What is the proportion of the red areas to the large square?

ANSWER: PAGE 119

All young children, when playing, go through the process of trying to fit a round peg into a square hole. They soon correct their mistake, but what if they didn't have to?

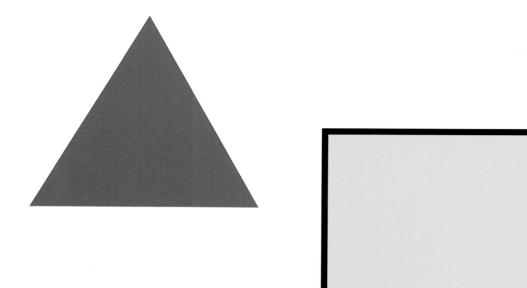

▲ TRIANGLE IN A SQUARE

What is the smallest equilateral triangle that can be inscribed in a unit square (so that its three vertices will lie on the sides of the square)?

And the largest?

ANSWER: PAGE 119

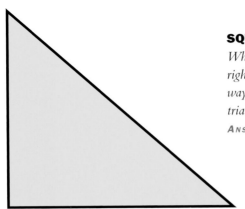

SQUARES IN A RIGHT TRIANGLE

What is the largest square that will fit into a right isosceles triangle, and how many different ways are there to place that square in the triangle?

ANSWER: PAGE *120*

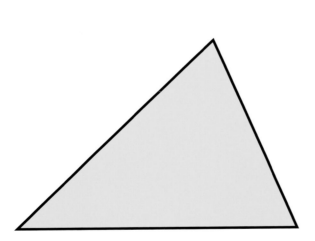

RECTANGLE IN A TRIANGLE

What is the largest rectangle that will fit in a given triangle?

ANSWER: PAGE *120*

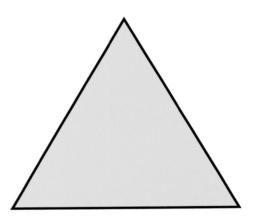

SQUARES IN A TRIANGLE

What is the largest square that will fit into an equilateral triangle, and how many different ways are there to place that square in the triangle?

ANSWER: PAGE *120*

Everyone enjoys a trip to the zoo, but did you ever consider the practicalities of housing the animals? Zookeepers have to keep track of much more than just feeding the animals.

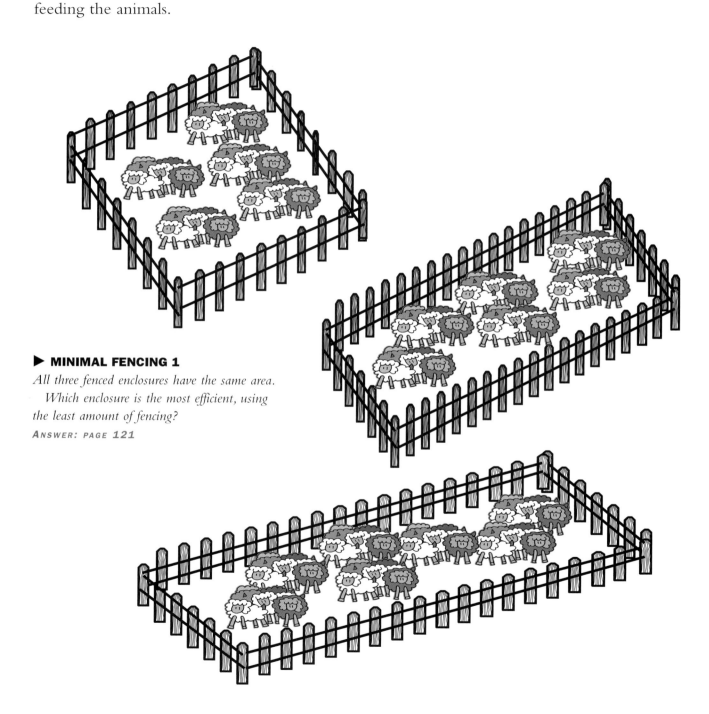

▶ MINIMAL FENCING 1

All three fenced enclosures have the same area.

Which enclosure is the most efficient, using the least amount of fencing?

ANSWER: PAGE **121**

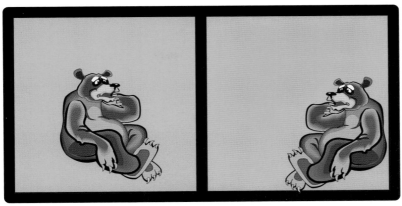

▲ MINIMAL FENCING 2

We have seen which shape is the minimal enclosure for all rectangles.

A somewhat more difficult problem is to find the best enclosure for two identical rectangles joined along their lengths.

Which is the enclosure that uses the least fencing here? The pictures are drawn to scale, and all have the same area.

In general, what is the most efficient enclosure for not just two, but infinitely many regions of identical area in the plane?

ANSWER: PAGE 121

The phrase "going around in circles" means that you're getting nowhere with the problem at hand. The puzzles on these pages show that old maxims are not necessarily true.

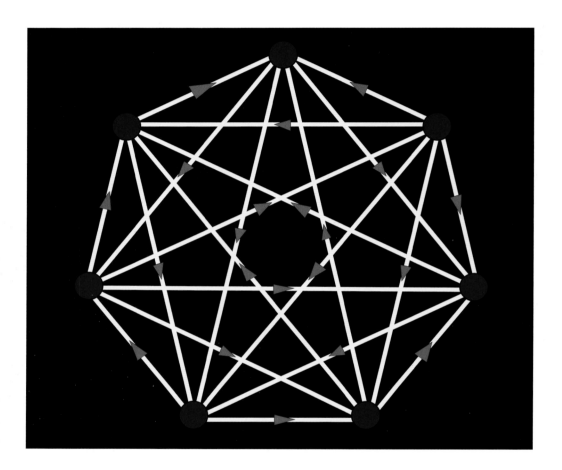

▲ DIGRAPH POLYGON

As we learned on page 42, a complete digraph is a graph in which every pair of points is joined by a path, and each path has an arrow on it.

One of the most surprising theorems involving complete digraphs is the "complete digraph theorem," which states: No matter how arrows are added to the lines of a complete digraph, there will always be a directed path that connects all points, visiting each point only once. Such a path is called a

Hamiltonian path. A special case of such a path is the one in which the path returns to its starting point. Such a path is called a Hamiltonian circuit.

The theorem guarantees a Hamiltonian path, but not a Hamiltonian circuit.

This is a complete digraph on 7 points. Can you find a Hamiltonian circuit, starting anywhere, visiting each point once, and ending where it started?

***ANSWER: PAGE* 121**

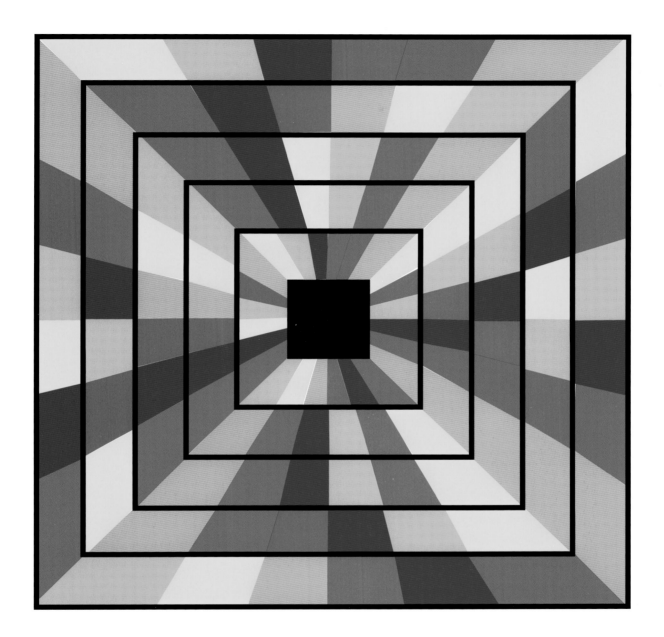

▲ NESTED SQUARES

*Just by looking, can you tell whether you can nest the five square frames
so as to obtain a pattern in which six radial lines of solid colors are
formed on each side of the squares?*

ANSWER: PAGE 121

Most people would be tempted to eat a box of chocolates before they would even consider rearranging them geometrically. But then of course they would deprive themselves of a perfectly good puzzle!

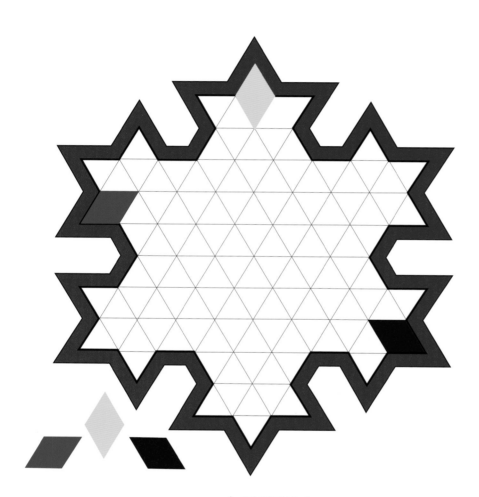

▲ PACKING CALISSONS

Calissons are French candies in the shape of diamonds composed of two equilateral triangles, packed in boxes of different shapes. Puzzles involving calissons are based on packing triangular grids with calissons.

Since each calisson occupies two triangles, the basic requirement of such grids is to have an even number of triangles.

But is this sufficient? Can every triangular grid composed of an even number of triangles be covered with calissons?

Can you fill the star-shaped box with calissons?

ANSWER: PAGE *122*

▼ OPAQUE SQUARE

Opaque fences are minimal barriers that block any straight line of sight passing through a given figure.

R. Honsberger, in 1978, introduced the "opaque square" or "opaque fences" problem, generalized to opaque regular polygons and opaque cube problems by Martin Gardner and Ian Stewart.

What will be the shortest total length of fence that will block any straight line passing through a square of unit side?

The fence can be composed of any shape, straight or curved, and can be more than one piece.

The most obvious solution would be to build a fence along the perimeter of the square as shown, which would have a length of 4 units, but a better solution would be to build the fence along three sides only, reducing the length to 3 units.

Can you build a shorter fence?

ANSWER: PAGE 122

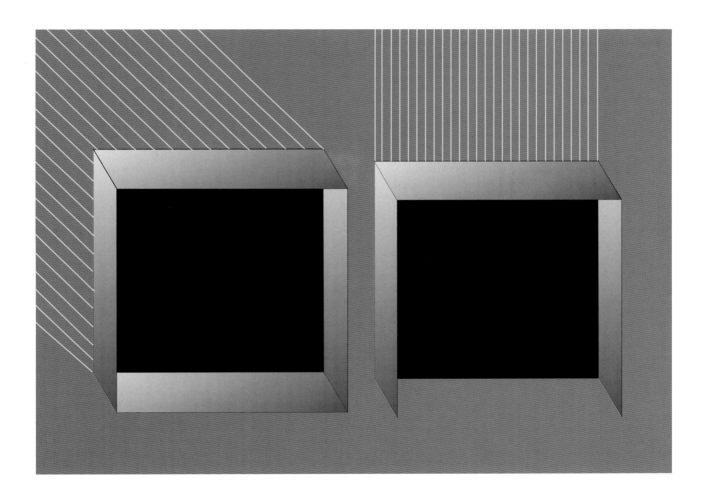

Mathematicians are fascinated with triangles because of the never-ending variety of places in which they appear, and, especially as we see here, the complex shapes they create.

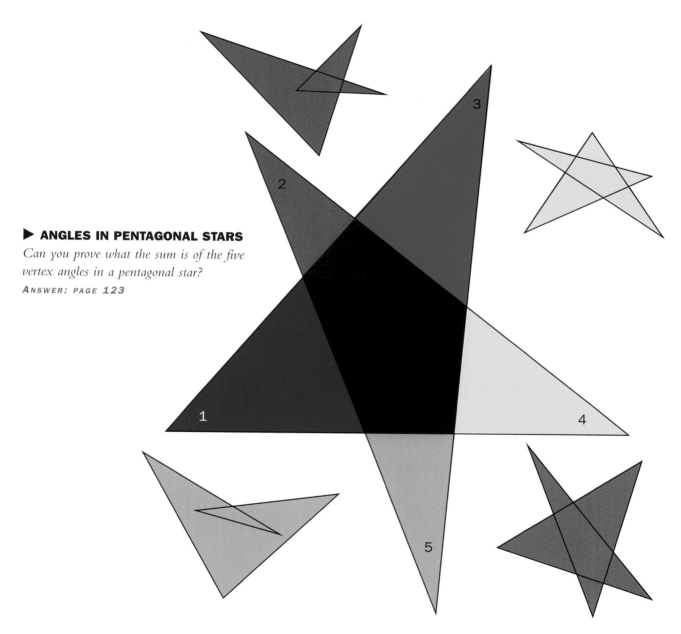

► ANGLES IN PENTAGONAL STARS

Can you prove what the sum is of the five vertex angles in a pentagonal star?

ANSWER: PAGE **123**

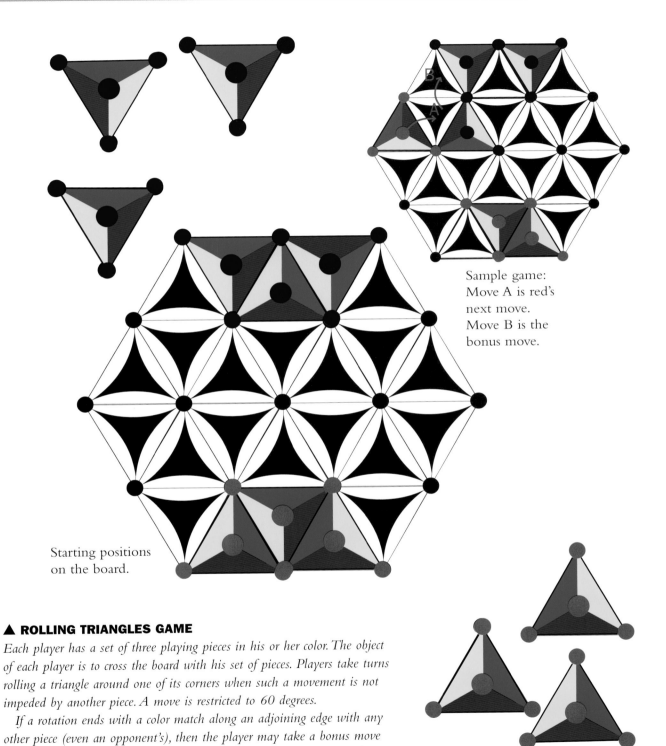

Sample game:
Move A is red's
next move.
Move B is the
bonus move.

Starting positions
on the board.

▲ ROLLING TRIANGLES GAME

Each player has a set of three playing pieces in his or her color. The object of each player is to cross the board with his set of pieces. Players take turns rolling a triangle around one of its corners when such a movement is not impeded by another piece. A move is restricted to 60 degrees.

If a rotation ends with a color match along an adjoining edge with any other piece (even an opponent's), then the player may take a bonus move (see sample game above). If that move results in another match, another bonus move may be taken, and so on.

Which do you think is more difficult? Establishing a variety of ways to divide a shape or uncovering a jumble of delineated areas? The problems on these pages will help you find out.

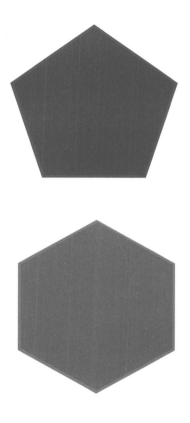

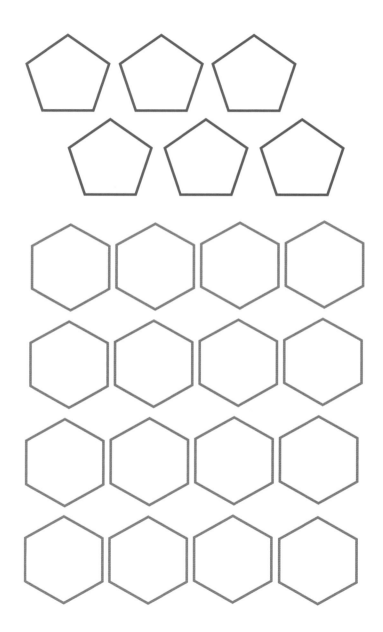

▶ TRIANGULATION

In how many ways can you cut a regular pentagon and regular hexagon into triangles, with straight cuts from corner to corner, without any intersections of the cutting lines?

Rotations and reflections are to be considered different for this problem, also called Euler's polygon division problem.

ANSWER: PAGE **123**

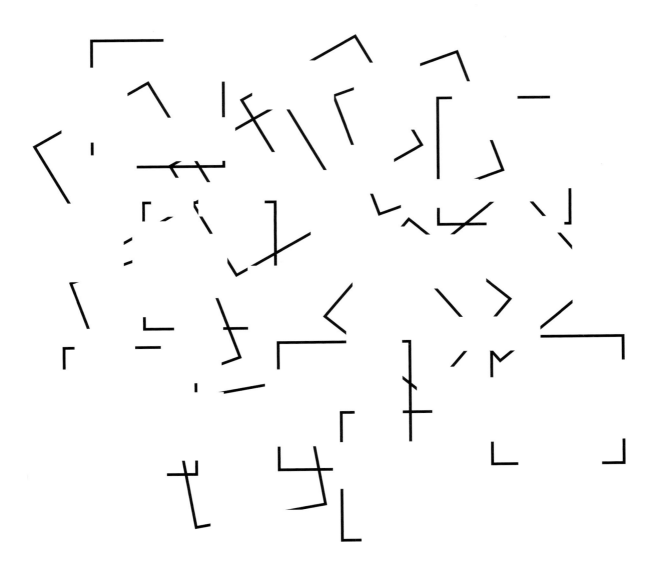

▲ SQUARE COUNT

A white mask of unknown shape has been placed over a collection of squares of equal size, and no square has been completely covered.

*   What is the number of squares?*

ANSWER: PAGE 124

Seemingly random occurences such as cracks in mud or the growth of soap bubbles can be explained by mathematics. Unconvinced? Read on.

✳ Branched structures

A soap film demonstrates cellular systems, which are constrained toward a minimum area of interface. A quite different type of structure is illustrated by a common tree or riverbed. Such a structure occurs in nature whenever a protuberance has an advantage over adjacent areas in getting more matter, heat, light or some other requisite for growth. Similar structures occur in solids under stress, cracks in mud, electric discharges, corrosion, and crystal growth.

All such structures start from a point and grow linearly, but they eventually stop as the branches interfere with others already present.

Do the cracks tend to intersect at any particular angle? Do the "islands" created by the cracks tend to have a certain geometric form?

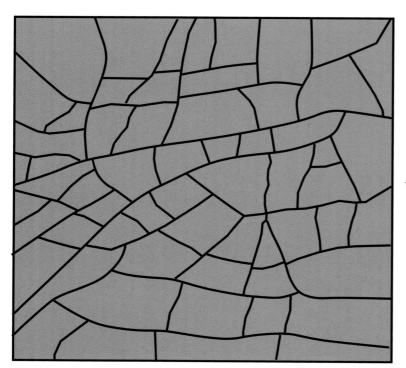

◀ CRACKS IN MUD
Just by observing the network of cracked mud at left, can you determine which was the initial crack in the network?
ANSWER: PAGE *124*

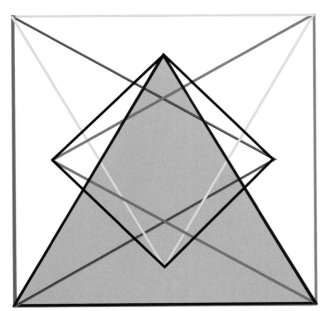

The Kurschak tile is shown by the black line

▶ DODECAGON AREA

Four equilateral triangles (red, green, yellow and blue) are drawn inwards from the outer square. By connecting their points, an inner square is formed (in black). When the midpoints of this square and the intersections of the sides of the triangles are joined, a regular dodecagon is formed, as shown. This square is called the Kurschak tile, and it is used to prove the Kurschak theorem, which shows that the area of a regular dodecagon inscribed in a circle of unit radius is three.

Just by looking at the tile, right, can you prove the area of the black-edged dodecagon in relation to the Kurschak tile?

ANSWER: PAGE 124

Cut a square in half, and you can get two triangles. Keep cutting, and you can get more—like a magician who keeps producing doves. See if you can work some magic on these triangles.

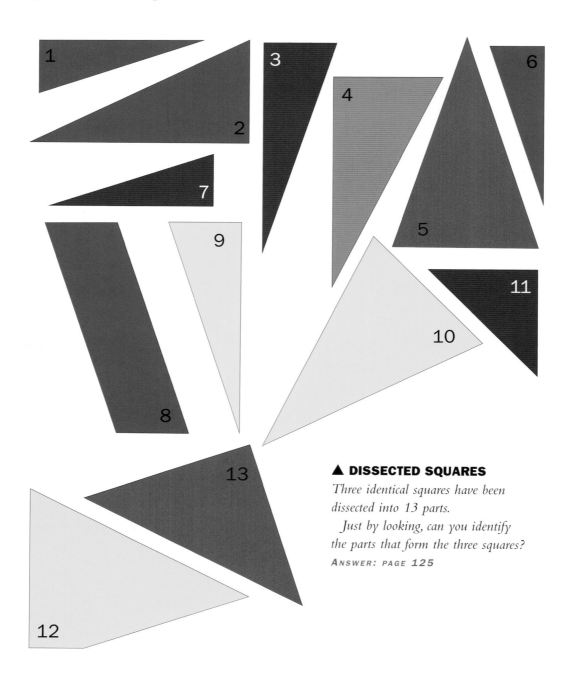

▲ DISSECTED SQUARES

Three identical squares have been dissected into 13 parts.

Just by looking, can you identify the parts that form the three squares?

ANSWER: PAGE **125**

◄ SQUARE CRISSCROSS

How many different patterns can you make if you color pairs of opposite sides and opposite corners, using four different colors for each square?

A sample coloring is shown at left.

Rotations of the squares are not considered to be different solutions.

ANSWER: PAGE 125

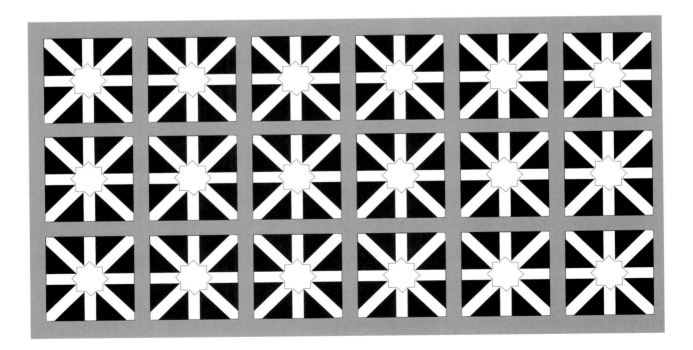

There are patterns all around us, whether we look for them deliberately or discover them by accident. Some of the most important scientific discoveries have been accompanied by beautiful patterns.

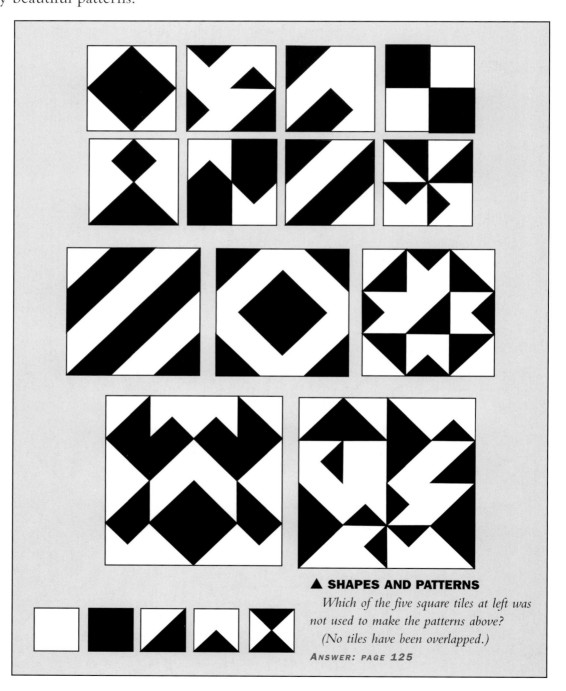

▲ SHAPES AND PATTERNS

Which of the five square tiles at left was not used to make the patterns above?
(No tiles have been overlapped.)

ANSWER: PAGE **125**

▼ PET SHOP

Sixteen aquariums with four types of fishes, each in four colors, are arranged in a pet shop in a 4-by-4 arrangement as shown. Ultimately the pet shop owner decided to create a more aesthetic display and rearranged the fishes in the same aquariums but so that there were four different fishes in four different colors in every horizontal row and vertical column.

Can you work out how he did it?

ANSWER: PAGE 126

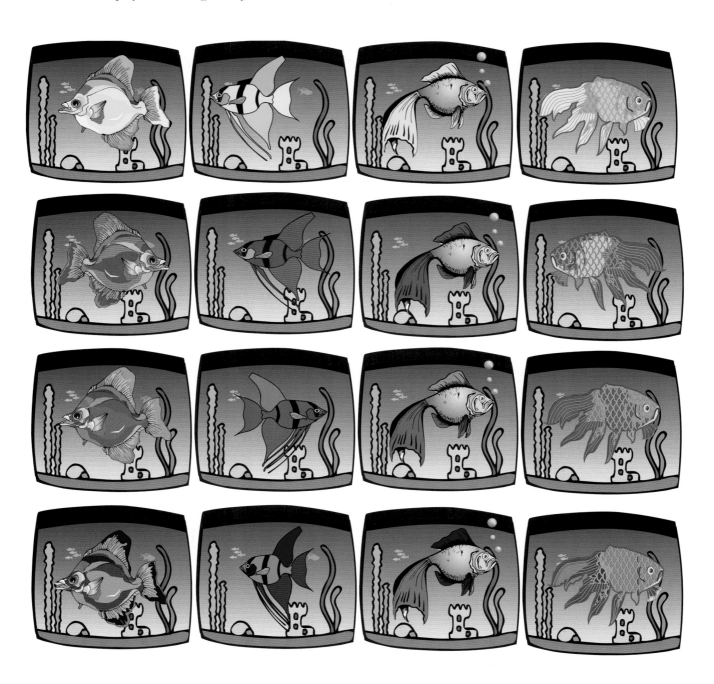

Visualizing the answer to a problem involving symmetry may at first seem relatively tricky. However, don't be tempted to use a mirror—there are ways of working it out unaided.

◄ **SYMMETRY LINES**
Which of the five patterns do not have eight lines of symmetry?
ANSWER: PAGE **127**

A drop of water contains several thousand million million atoms. Each atom is about one hundred-millionth of an inch in diameter. Here we marvel at the minute delicacy of the workmanship. But this is not the limit. Within the atom are the much smaller electrons pursuing orbits, like planets around the sun, in a space which relative to their size is no less roomy than the solar system."

Sir Arthur Eddington,
"Stars and Atoms," 1927

▲ RED DROP

A drop of water, dyed red, falls into a bowl of water. After it falls into the bowl, will you ever be able to see the red drop again?

ANSWER: PAGE *128*

✳ Fluid Mechanics

The general term "fluid" includes any substance that has no rigidity. Fluids do not have any definite length or shape. Thus liquids and gases are fluid; they have only volume. A further distinction can be made between liquids and gases: A liquid has a surface. In other words, the binding forces between the molecules of liquids are sufficient to give a definite volume to the liquid. Gases have no such volume and will expand to fill any container uniformly. Fluids are more easily compressed than solids, and gases are more easily compressed than liquids.

Fluid mechanics is an integrated part of some basic machines, as well as a fundamental part of some of the most advanced kinds of computers.

Fluid mechanics has several subdivisions, corresponding to the kind of physical problems studied. They include the theory of gases, hydrostatics (liquids at rest), hydrodynamics (the motion of fluids), aerostatics (gases at rest), and hydrodynamics (the motion of gases).

Liquids at rest make a good starting point for the study of forces in general. This is because the forces due to the weight of fluids are relatively simple.

And to finish, a couple of science-related questions. Time to put your white lab coat on....

▲ BURNING CANDLE

A candle is placed in a dish of water, lit, and hermetically covered by a bottle as shown.

Can you predict what the consequences of this experiment will be?

ANSWER: PAGE **128**

▶ CHEMISTRY EXPERIMENT

The six flasks can be filled with 7, 9, 19, 20, 21, and 22 units of liquid. To initiate the experiment, the chemist has to fill some flasks with red liquid, then some with blue liquid, leaving one flask empty. When the correct flasks are filled, he will have used twice as much blue liquid as red liquid.

Can you tell which flasks are to be filled with red and which with blue liquid and which flask will be the one left empty?

ANSWER: PAGE 128

▼ FACE FINDER (page 6)

It shouldn't be difficult to find the sulking face near the top right corner.

The human perceptual system is designed to detect an item that stands out as different in a multitude of identical elements in a system, without the need for a systematic search. This principle is used in the design of instrument panels for aircrafts, cars, etc. Under normal circumstances, in which all the indicators point in the same direction, any change is easily spotted.

▼ GIRLS AND BOYS IN A ROW (page 6)

▼ TESSELLATION PATTERNS (page 7)

Although it seems like you need two shapes for each diagram, only one shape is needed in either case. For example, in the upper diagram you could start with a yellow background then use many copies of the purple piece shown here.

▼ BOWLING LINEUP (page 8)

You have six people to choose from; someone has to go first. Someone then goes second, with five people remaining to choose from. Someone now goes third, with four people left. There are three choices for the final person.

Therefore, that's $6 \times 5 \times 4 \times 3 = 360$ possible lineups.

▼ ACROBATS 1 (page 9)

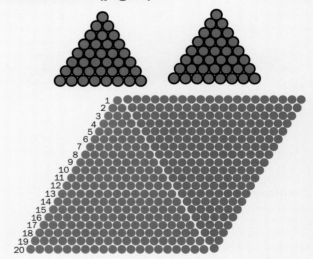

▲ ACROBATS 2 (page 9)

Imagine we had two pyramids, but one was upside down (see above). It's easy to see this is as a slanted rectangle (or parallelogram) of 20 rows containing 21 acrobats each. That's 420 acrobats in the two pyramids. Therefore, one pyramid contains 210 acrobats.

▼ ARCHIMEDES' PRINCIPLE (page 10)

If the displaced water were the same in both cases, the crown would be proven solid gold.

But this was not the case. The crown displaced more water, proving that the crown was alloyed with a less dense metal than gold, the volume of which is greater than the volume of solid gold.

The crown turned out to be a fake, and Archimedes' fame continued as he made many other discoveries.

The discovery of the fact that a body in liquid gains a lift (i.e., it becomes lighter) due to the upward force called buoyancy, which is equal to the mass of the displaced liquid, established the science of hydrostatics.

Ever since Archimedes' discovery, this method has been used to assay metals, identify jewels, and measure the density of materials. We can compare the mass of a substance with the mass of an equal volume of water by means of Archimedes' principle.

The ratio of these masses is called the specific gravity of the body:

$$\text{specific gravity} = \frac{\text{mass of object}}{\text{mass of equal volume of water}}$$

▼ LIQUID BALANCE—BUOYANCY (page 11)

The submerged weight is subject to a buoyant force equal to the weight of the volume of water displaced by the weight. You were most likely tempted to say that to restore equilibrium this weight should be added to the pan with the stand.

But is it enough?

According to Newton's third law, the force with which the water in the container acts on the submerged weight is exactly equal to the force with which the weight acts on the water in the opposite direction.

Hence, as the weight on the pan with the stand decreases, the weight on the pan with the container increases.

To restore the balance, a weight equal to 2W has to be added, where W is the weight of the volume of water displaced by the submerged weight.

▶ PAIRING PATTERNS (pages 12 and 13)

1	2	3	4	5
6	7	8	9	10
11	12	13	14	15
16	17	18	19	20
21	22	23	24	25
26	27	28	29	30

5	27	13	28	8
30	11	18	3	20
23	16	7	15	29
2	17	10	6	26
9	14	22	1	24
21	4	19	25	12

▼ THREE-COURSE MENU (page 16)

You have two choices for the first course. Whichever you choose, you have three further choices for the second course. For each of the six choices you have two choices for the dessert.

The solution is the product of the number of choices:

$2 \times 3 \times 2 = 12$ three-course meals.

▼ LOTTO (page 17)

The number of ways is given by the general formula (seen on page 15) of the number of combinations of n objects (in this case, numbers) taken k at a time.

$$_nC_k = \frac{n!}{k!\,(n-k)!} = \frac{54!}{6!\,(54-6)!}$$

$$= \frac{54 \times 53 \times 52 \times \ldots \times 3 \times 2 \times 1}{(6 \times 5 \times 4 \times 3 \times 2 \times 1) \times (48 \times 47 \times 46 \times \ldots \times 3 \times 2 \times 1)}$$

$$= 25{,}827{,}165$$

▼ ROUND TABLE (page 18)

There is only one such arrangement, as shown below.

For a larger number of couples, more solutions are possible, as shown here for up to 10 couples:

n = 3 1
n = 4 2
n = 5 13
n = 6 80
n = 7 579
n = 8 4738
n = 9 43387
n = 10 439792

In recreational math literature this problem is known as the Ménage Problem.

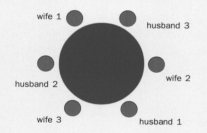

wife 1 husband 3
husband 2 wife 2
wife 3 husband 1

▼ ANIMAL CAROUSELS (page 20)

There are four different solutions, one of them shown.

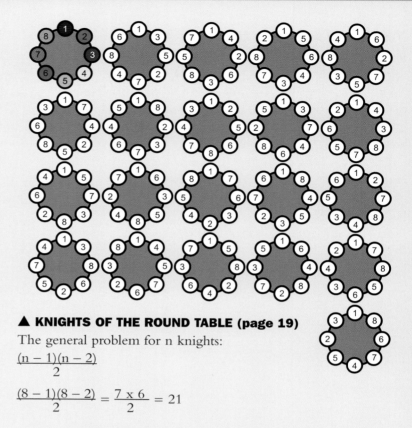

▲ KNIGHTS OF THE ROUND TABLE (page 19)

The general problem for n knights:

$$\frac{(n-1)(n-2)}{2}$$

$$\frac{(8-1)(8-2)}{2} = \frac{7 \times 6}{2} = 21$$

▼ ICE CREAM CONES (page 21)

There are six different ways the scoops can be ordered in the cone, or 3! (3 factorial), so the probability is 1 in 6 that you will get your cone just the way you like it.

◄ WHISPERING TUBES (page 22)

Sound travels in waves, just as light does, and it obeys the same laws of reflection too.

The children will best be able to hear each other when the two tubes are placed so that the angles between them and the wall are equal.

The beam of sound is reflected off the wall at an angle equal to the one it strikes at.

▼ PASCAL'S PRINCIPLE (page 23)

It must be remembered that while the hydraulic press enables us to exert enormous force, it is done at the expense of distance. Thus, with every unit of movement of the large piston there will be seven units of movement of the small piston.

The pressure used on the small cylinder is seven grams, and the weight that is lifted by this pressure is 49 grams, i.e., seven times as much.

▼ POLYGONS AND LINES (page 24)

Regular: 6, 12
Open: 1, 8
Closed: 2, 3, 4, 5, 6, 7, 9, 10, 11, 12
Simple: 4, 5, 6, 10, 11, 12
Complex: 2, 3, 7, 9
Compound: 3, 9
Convex: 5, 6, 10, 12
Non-convex: 1, 2, 3, 4, 7, 8, 9, 11

▼ CROSSED POLYGONS (page 25)

Puzzle 1

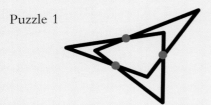

Puzzle 4

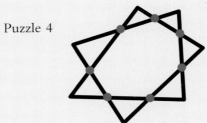

Puzzles 2 and 3 are impossible.

▶ CHORD INTERSECTIONS (page 26)

The common chords of three intersecting circles always meet at a point. Therefore, with three sets of three circles, the three points will form a triangle.

▼ TO INFINITY WITH CIRCLES (page 27)

One orange circle is half the radius of the larger yellow circle, so therefore (due to the formula for a circle's area) it has one quarter of the area. However, there are two orange circles, so together the orange circles enclose half the area of the yellow circle—including all the colored circles they enclose. The same argument can be repeated for all the other colors.

So the areas of the circles (counting the enclosed areas) are:

Yellow circle	1 unit area
Orange circles	½ unit area
Red circles	¼ unit area
Green circles	⅛ unit area
Blue circles	¹⁄₁₆ unit area
Black circles	¹⁄₃₂ unit area

▼ SEE THROUGH (page 28)

A vertical red and green zigzag pattern as shown.

▼ ARCHIMEDES' STOMACHION (page 29)

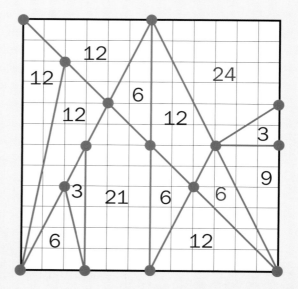

Piece number	1	2	3	4	5	6	7	8	9	10	11	12	13	14
Area (square units)	12	12	24	12	6	12	3	21	6	6	6	3	9	12

▼ POLYGON-STAR TRANSFORMATIONS 1 (page 30)

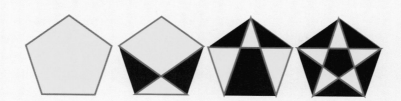

◀ POLYGON-STAR TRANSFORMATIONS 2 (page 31)

▼ POLYGON-STAR TRANSFORMATIONS 3 (page 32)

Here are 23 different symmetrical irregular heptagonal stars that can be drawn on the regular heptagon. Did you find at least 14 of these?

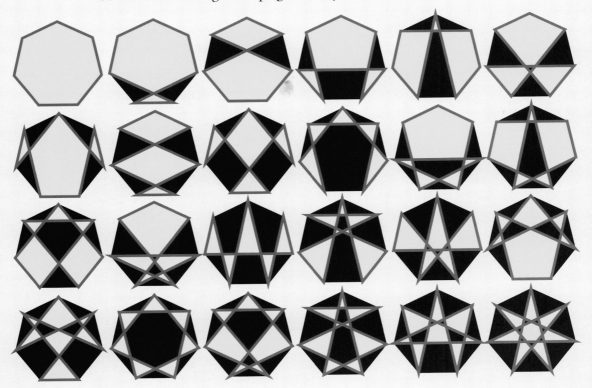

▼ **TWO COLOR BEAD STRINGS (page 33)**

There are four possible couplets: Red-Red; Red-Blue; Blue-Blue; Blue-Red.

The longest two-color string in which no couplet is repeated has a length of five:

There are eight possible triplets; the longest two-color string in which no triplet is repeated has a length of 10:

▼ **STAR HEXAGONS (page 34)**

The irregular hexagonal star appears only once, while all the others are in pairs.

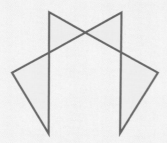

▼ **RAINBOW LOOP (page 35)**

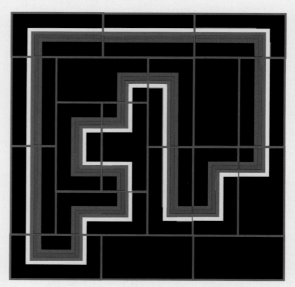

▼ FREDKIN'S AUTOMATON (page 36)

The initial pattern of three red cells transforms over four generations into four identical replicas, as shown.

Fredkin's cellular automaton has a fascinating property. It is a self-replicating machine. Every initial configuration will, after a certain number of generations, replicate itself into 4, 16, and 64 identical copies of itself.

Edward Fredkin of MIT created this system in 1960.

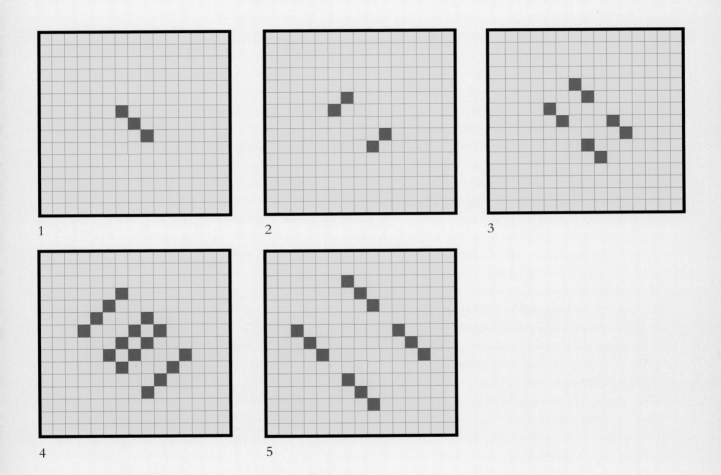

1

2

3

4

5

▼ OVERHAND KNOT (page 37)

The knot will disappear. This also happens when the rope is passed through only once.

The end of the rope must pass through the loop three times to form another knot again, which will not be exactly the same as the original. It will be its mirror image.

▼ MINIMAL NEIGHBORHOOD (page 38)

For any number of even buildings along a straight street, any building between the two middle buildings will have a minimal sum of the distances to all your friends.

For any odd number of buildings the center building will be the spot.

This problem was introduced by J. Butcharts and Leo Moser in 1952.

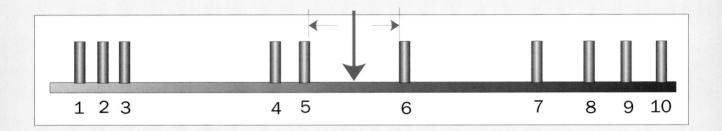

▶ SOAP RINGS (page 39)

The minimal surface formed is called a catenoid.

▶ LEFT-RIGHT-HANDED (page 40)

N is the number of schoolchildren who are both left- and right-handed.

Seven times as many are left-handed only, and nine times as many are right-handed only.

$N + 6N + 8N = 15N$ is the total number of children.

The proportion of right-handed children to the entire classroom is 9N to 15N, or $3/5$, which is more than half.

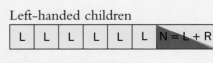

▼ TWO MILLION DOTS (page 41)

We can choose a point outside the circle from which a rotating line sweeps the circle in one direction while we count the dots that the line crosses until we reach 1 million. At this position the line divides the circle with one million dots on each side of the line.

If, by bad luck, the line sweeps over two dot and jumps from 999,999 to 1,000,001, we choose another point outside the circle and try again. The process always works eventually. This is a simplified version of a proof known as the pancake theorem.

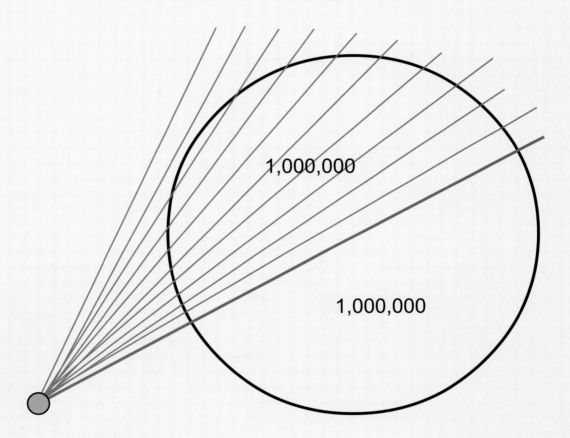

1,000,000

1,000,000

▼ DIGRAPH ARROW TRIANGLES (page 42)

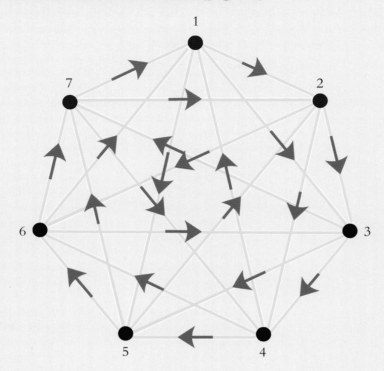

▼ CHESSCUBE (page 43)

There are $8 \times 8 \times 8$ individual cubes.
There are $7 \times 7 \times 7$ cubes of 2×2.
There are $6 \times 6 \times 6$ cubes of 3×3.
And so on until one large cube of 8×8.

Total $= 8^3 + 7^3 + 6^3 + 5^3 + 4^3 + 3^3 + 2^3 + 1^3 = 1296$.

There is an alternative formula that can be used to get to the same answer:

Sum of cubes from 1 to n

$$= \left[\frac{n}{2} \times (n + 1) \right]^2$$
$$= 1296 \text{ when } n = 8$$

▶ RED-BLUE-GREEN RING (PAGE 44)

Red has the greatest area (19 units), followed by green (18 units), then blue (17 units).

The puzzle is based on Bonaventura Cavalieri's (1598–1647) theorem: Two or more triangles with a common base and equal altitudes have equal areas.

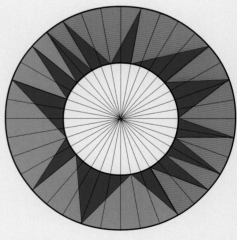

▼ MENTAL BLOCKS (page 45)

The Heesch's tile, on which this puzzle is based, does not allow the tiling of the plane, yet it can be completely surrounded by seven congruent tiles.

▼ CAT IN A FLAP (page 46)

Red door 7 and blue door 2 are the right doors.

Our judgment is generally influenced by the background figure to make us choose a squarer shape than the actual one in the original.

▼ CON-NECTION (page 47)

One of many possible solutions.

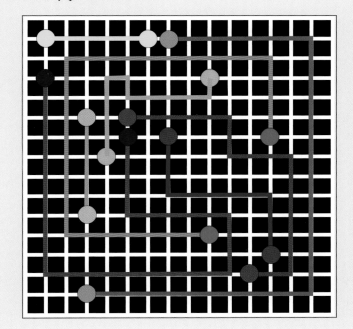

▼ PASSWORD (page 48)

Puzzle 1:

26 choices for each letter and 10 choices for each digit:

$P = 26 \times 26 \times 26 \times 10 \times 10 = 26^3 \times 10^2$

$= 1,757,600$

Puzzle 2:

$P = 26 \times 25 \times 24 \times 10 \times 9 = 1,404,000$

Puzzle 3:

$P = 1 \times 25 \times 24 \times 10 \times 9 = 54,000$

▼ CAMOUFLAGE (page 49)

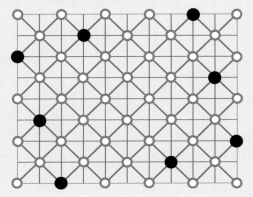

▶ **PEGBOARD CLOSED POLYGONS 1 (page 50)**

No matter how you draw the polygons on a 3-by-3 pegboard, two pegs will always be left unoccupied, while on a 5-by-5 pegboard, one peg will always be left out. On the 4-by-4 pegboard no peg is left unused.

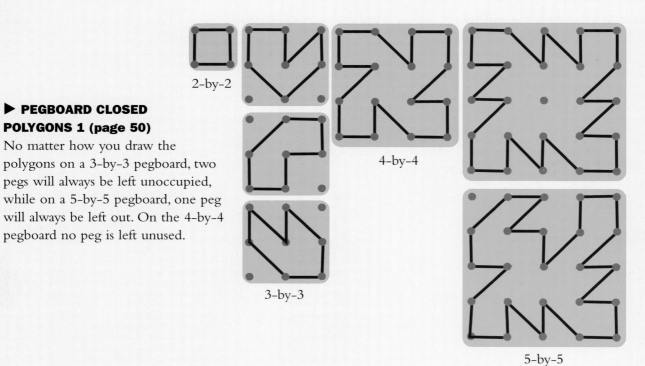

2-by-2

3-by-3

4-by-4

5-by-5

▶ **PEGBOARD CLOSED POLYGONS 2 (page 52)**

Other solutions are possible.

6-by-6

7-by-7

8-by-8

9-by-9

▼ **PEGBOARD CLOSED POLYGONS 3 (page 52)**

n = 2

n = 3

n = 4

n = 5

n = 6

n = 7

n = 8

▶ **PEGBOARD CLOSED POLYGONS 4 (page 53)**

Other answers are possible.

n = 2

n = 3

n = 4

n = 5

n = 6

▼ OVERLAPPING HEXAGONS (page 54)

Combined, the four green hexagons have the same area as the red hexagon; if you double the length of the side of a hexagon, you quadruple the area.

When you overlap the green and red hexagons, notice that you are reducing the area of the green and red areas by the same amount. Therefore, there is still no difference between the green and red areas, no matter where the green hexagons are positioned.

▼ TRIANGLE STICKS (PAGE 55)

There are 20 ways of selecting three of the six sticks. You can work this out mathematically using one of the formulas we have previously encountered:

$$_nC_r = 6! \,/\, (3! \times 3!)$$
$$= 6 \times 5 \times 4 \times 3 \times 2 \times 1 \,/\, [(3 \times 2 \times 1) \times (3 \times 2 \times 1)]$$
$$= 720 \,/\, (6 \times 6)$$
$$= 20$$

Of these 20 arrangements, a triangle cannot be formed using combinations of 3-4-7, 3-4-8, and 3-5-8 because the sum of the two shorter sides must be greater than the longest side. So there are 17 valid combinations.

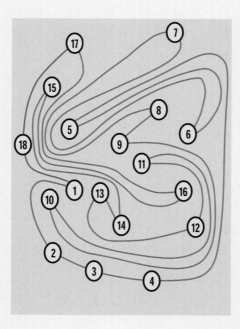

◀ CON-NEXT (PAGE 56)

Although we've chosen 18 points for this puzzle, you could join up any number of points because essentially you are drawing a distorted circle.

▲ PEGBOARD QUADRILATERALS (PAGE 57)

Puzzle 1) There are 16 distinct quadrilaterals.
Puzzle 2) There are 10 different ways to divide the
pegboard into quarters of equal area.

▼ HOW MANY SQUARES 1? (PAGE 58)

23 squares.

▼ HOW MANY SQUARES 2? (PAGE 59)

50 squares.

▶ EQUAL AREAS AND PERIMETERS (PAGE 61)

The four shapes on the left have the same area. The shapes on the right have equal perimeters. The two circles are identical and have the same area and perimeter. The same perimeters in the other three shapes on the right all enclose a smaller area than the other three shapes. (The shapes here are not to scale.)

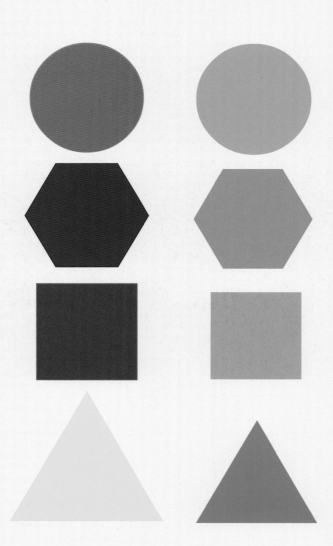

▼ PEGBOARD SHAPES 1 (PAGE 62)

The answer is 7.5 grid unit squares.

To solve these, first count the number of undivided unit squares within the area enclosed by the rubber band. The remaining areas can be divided into triangles, which can in turn be seen as half of a rectangle. Thus, the three squares inside the first rubber band are surrounded by half a 1 × 2 rectangle, half a 1 × 3 rectangle, and a half a 1 × 4 rectangle. Adding these areas (3 + 1 + 1.5 + 2) gives the total area of 7.5.

▼ PEGBOARD SHAPES 2 (PAGE 62)

The areas of the other four shapes are: 17, 9, 10, 16 unit squares respectively.

The method used for puzzle 1 works well with simple shapes such as these. For more complex shapes, "Pick's theorem" makes finding the solution very easy.

All one has to do is to count the number of points (pegs) inside the closed polygon (N), and the number of points on the boundary line (B). The total area is:

$$N + \frac{B}{2} - 1$$

You can check the validity of this formula for our puzzles.

▼ HOW MANY TRIANGLES? (PAGE 63)

1) 1 triangle   4) 27 triangles
2) 5 triangles   5) 48 triangles
3) 13 triangles   6) 78 triangles

For even values of n the total number of triangles will be:

$$\frac{n(n + 2)(2n + 1)}{8}$$

For odd values of n the formula is:

$$\frac{n(n + 2)(2n + 1) - 1}{8}$$

If your answer for n = 4 was 26, remember you must consider larger triangles that point down the page.

▼ PEGGING SQUARES (page 64)

The solution is unique.

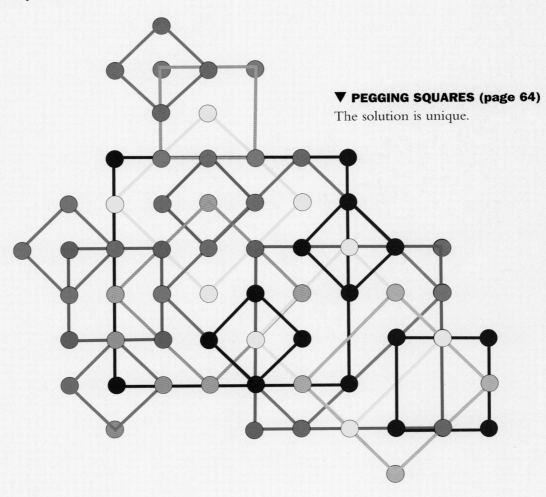

▶ CHVATAL ART GALLERY (page 65)

A theorem to solve the art gallery problem was suggested by Vasek Chvatal and Steve Frisk:

Triangulate the whole layout and color the vertices of each triangle in three different colors, using the same three colors for each triangle. The cameras should be placed at the points that have the color that appears the fewest times.

This theorem provides the theoretical maximum number of the required cameras, but it does not guarantee the possible minimum.

In our case triangulation gives six cameras as a maximum, but in practice this number can be reduced to four as shown.

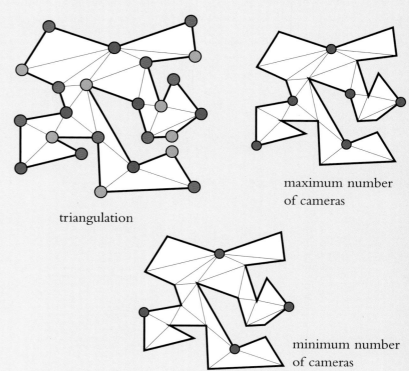

triangulation

maximum number of cameras

minimum number of cameras

◀ ANGLES IN A TRIANGLE (page 66)

By folding in the vertices of a triangle as shown, it can be transformed into a rectangle; this makes the three angles of the triangle lie on a straight line, adding up to an angle of 180 degrees.

Geometry of space can be Euclidean, spherical, or hyperbolic. The angles of a triangle on the spherical surface add up to over 180 degrees, and on the hyperbolic surface (or saddle surface) to less than 180 degrees.

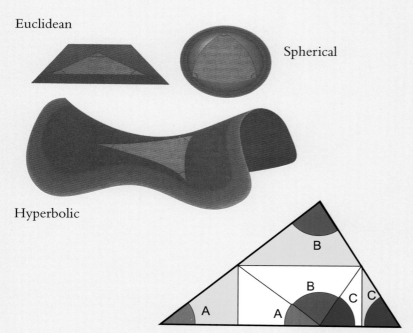

Euclidean

Spherical

Hyperbolic

▶ **THE BOOMERANG PROBLEM**
(page 67)

By filling the dents the figure becomes
a regular hexagon of the same area.
Area of the hexagon
= 6 × triangle

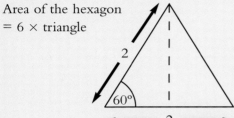

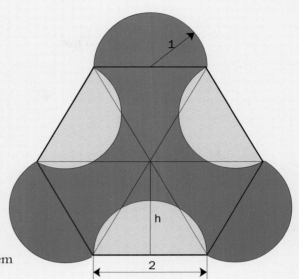

= $6 \times \frac{1}{2} \times$ base × height

= $6 \times (\frac{1}{2} \times 2 \times (\sqrt{2^2 - 1^2})$ by the Pythagorean theorem

▶ **JOINING SQUARES AND TRIANGLES**
(page 68)

13 triangles and 7 squares are needed to
create a convex polygon of 11 sides. You
may have had some difficulty constructing
it if you assumed that the sides of the 11-
sided polygon had to be identical.

Any convex pentagon formed by
triangles can be used as the core of an
11-sided convex polygon.

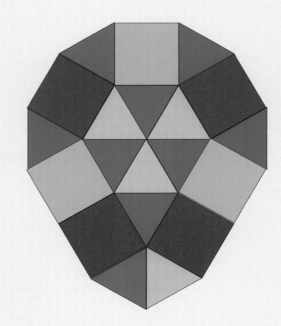

▶ LADYBUG COLLECTION (page 69)

Each of the 19 ladybugs is in a separate compartment.

In general, the maximum number of regions of three intersecting triangles is 19.

This can be easily proven. Two overlapping triangles can form no more than 7 separate regions. Each side of a third triangle can intersect a maximum of 4 lines, forming 3 new regions, a total of 12 new regions.

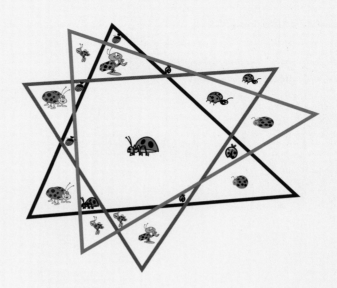

▼ SHORTEST ROUTES IN A HEXAGON (page 70)

Two possible solutions for six points at the vertices of a regular hexagon of unit side.

The shortest way there is to connect the vertices of a regular hexagon is to use five of the six sides, which has a total length of 5 units.

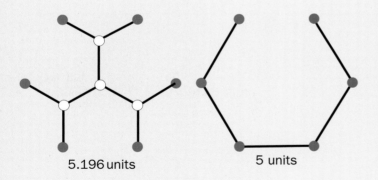

5.196 units   5 units

▼ FOUR-TOWN SPANNING TREES (page 71)

The third diagram in the top row has the shortest total road length.

In 1968, Edgar Gilbert and Henry Pollak at Bell Labs theorized that no matter how the towns are situated, the maximum savings by adding Steiner points would be 13.34% (Steiner ratio conjecture). After 23 years this was proven by Ding Zhu Du at Princeton and Frank Hwang at Bell Labs.

The problems of finding the minimal routes between a large number of points is extremely difficult. Soap bubbles seem to "know" all the principles involved, and simple models dipped into soap solution often give answers to complex problems in no time.

▼ THE TURN PUZZLE (page 72)

Each piece has a circle in the same color around which it revolves. Giving each piece a 180° turn clockwise will reveal the name of the puzzle, as shown below.

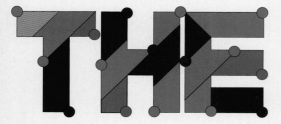

▼ HIDDEN FIGURES (page 73)

Each outline can be found twice.

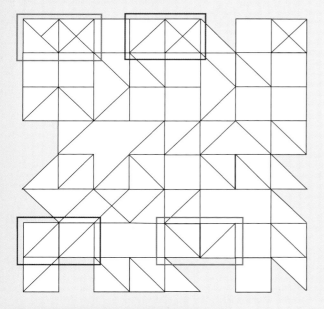

▼ TRIANGLE TRISECTED (page 74)

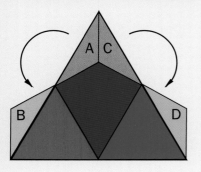

▼ SQUARE GRID (page 75)

The red areas represent 44% of the large square.

First note that all the vertical lines are parallel. Because the area of a parallelogram is the same as a rectangle of the same base and height, we can redraw the grid with the lines perfectly vertical without affecting the area. (If you like, we are correcting the "lean"). Now it's just a simple matter of counting the squares. We can then easily see that four-ninths (44.44%) of the area is red.

▼ TRIANGLE IN A SQUARE (page 76)

The smallest equilateral triangle:
side = 1
area ≈ 0.4330

The largest equilateral triangle:
side = 1.035
area ≈ 0.4641

The area of an equilateral triangle:

$$A = \frac{\sqrt{3}}{4}\ S^2$$

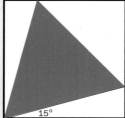

▶ SQUARES IN A RIGHT TRIANGLE (page 77)

The largest square that can be placed in a right isosceles triangle is shown in red; there is only one way it can be placed. The other square which can be inscribed on the hypotenuse of the right isosceles triangle (shown in green) is slightly smaller than the red square.

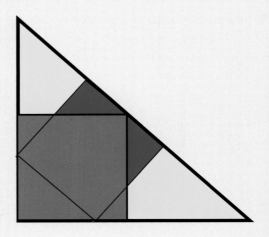

▶ RECTANGLE IN A TRIANGLE (page 77)

Connect the midpoints of any two sides to meet the third side perpendicularly as shown to create a maximum rectangle. There are three such rectangles (not necessarily of the same shape but of the same area) in any acute triangle. Right triangles have two (one of which is a square), and obtuse triangles only one, which rests on the side opposite the obtuse angle. The area of the maximum rectangle is half the triangle's area (Euclid, book 6.27), which can easily be demonstrated by paper folding.

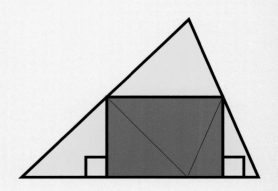

◀ SQUARES IN A TRIANGLE (page 77)

The largest possible square can fit into an equilateral triangle three ways, as shown.

The square's size is shown in relationship to a unit base.

▼ MINIMAL FENCING 1 (page 78)

The best rectangular enclosure is the square. It uses less fencing material than any other rectangular enclosure having the same area.

▼ MINIMAL FENCING 2 (page 79)

The double cage with the elephants is the best enclosure, using the least fencing for the walls of the double cage for the same area.

Not two squares, but two rectangles that are a third longer than wide, taking full advantage of the common fence that is part of both rectangles.

For example, for the two joined squares with sides of 6 cm, the enclosed area is 72 cm^2 and the fencing is 42 cm.

For the two rectangles with sides of 5.27 and 6.83, the area is the same as of the squares, but the total fencing is only 41.57 cm.

The answer to the final question is tiling by regular hexagons. The proof was provided in 1999, by Thomas Hales of the University of Michigan. This may partly explain why hexagons occur in nature, as in bees' honeycombs.

▼ DIGRAPH POLYGON (page 80)

A Hamiltonian circuit. Others are possible.

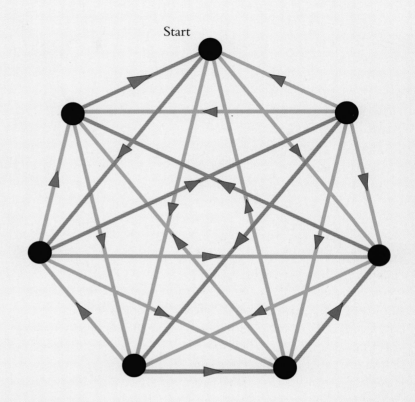

▶ NESTED SQUARES (page 81)

It cannot be done. The closest pattern is shown at right.

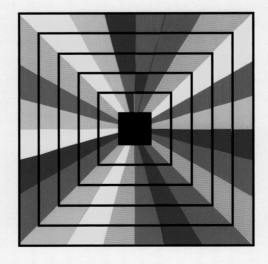

▶ PACKING CALISSONS (page 82)

One valid solution is shown below. There is an interesting theorem associated with packing calissons. Given any packing, it will not be possible to repack the box with a different number of any color of calisson.

In the case of this diagram, each color must always represent one-third of the total number of calissons in the box.

Using the diamond pieces you may notice an accompanying striking three-dimensional effect.

▼ OPAQUE SQUARE (page 83)

A shorter fence cannot consist of a single line, because the U-shape is the shortest single-line fence that contains all four corners.

The minimal Steiner tree (minimal surface) spanning four corners of a square creates a fence of 2.732 unit length, but it is not the shortest opaque square fence.

A fence of two disconnected parts can be reduced to about 2.639 unit lengths (believed to the best solution but not yet proven).

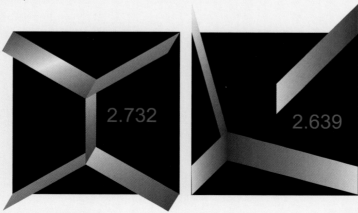

▼ **ANGLES IN PENTAGONAL STARS (page 84)**

The angles in a pentagonal star add up to 180 degrees.

No matter how a pentagonal star is drawn, and no matter how it is distorted, its five angles will always add up to 180 degrees.

You can check this by cutting out the angles of any star and gluing them together to define a straight line.

A similar proof can be obtained by rotating a matchstick in a pentagonal star. Place a matchstick along the horizontal line pointing left. Slide the match to the end of the line and turn it along the angle and repeat. At the end you will come back to the line you started from, with the matchstick pointing in the opposite direction, showing that it rotated 180 degrees.

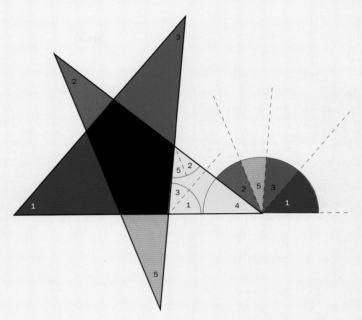

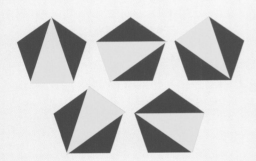

◀ **TRIANGULATION (page 86)**

In general, the number of different ways regular polygons can be divided into triangles is:

1, 2, 5, 14, 42, 132, 429, 1430, 4862, ...

These numbers are called Catalan numbers, after Eugene Catalan (1814–1894). They appear in many problems of combinatorics.

▶ SQUARE COUNT (page 87)

15 squares.

▼ CRACKS IN MUD (page 88)

The earliest crack is the one which extends fully across the square. It starts on the left side, about halfway down, and goes to the right side, about a third of the way down.

In the 1960s, James Neal of the U.S. Air Force Cambridge Research Laboratory concluded from his studies of mud cracks that as a rule the intersections are approximately perpendicular and the islands are four-sided. Geometric constraints influence the patterns found in cracked mud. The natural tendency is for the simplest of all networks to be formed—one in which there are only three edges meeting at each corner. Cracking is inevitably sequential rather than simultaneous. As a result, when a crack is formed, it will typically join an existing crack by forming a three-rayed intersection. The formation of a four-rayed intersection is highly unlikely, since it is improbable that two new cracks would intersect an existing crack from opposite sides at exactly the same point.

Usually it is possible to decide which crack appeared earlier and which later: The older of the two cracks passes right through the point of junction.

▼ DODECAGON AREA (page 89)

The tile is dissected into 16 equilateral triangles and 32 isosceles triangles with angles of 15, 15, and 150 degrees.

Four of the 16 equilateral triangles and 8 of the 32 isosceles triangles lie outside the dodecagon. Therefore the dodecagon has $\frac{3}{4}$ the area of the square. The square has an area of 4 (as it has been defined as circumscribing a circle of unit radius, hence has a side of 2), so the dodecagon's area is 3.

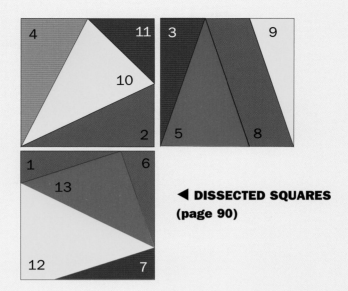

◀ **DISSECTED SQUARES**
(page 90)

▼ **SQUARE CRISSCROSS (page 91)**
There are 12 essentially different colorings as shown.

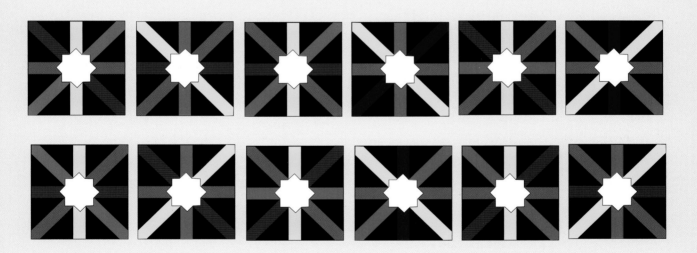

▶ **SHAPES AND PATTERNS (page 92)**
This square pattern is not used.

▼ **PET SHOP (page 93)**

Here is one possible solution.

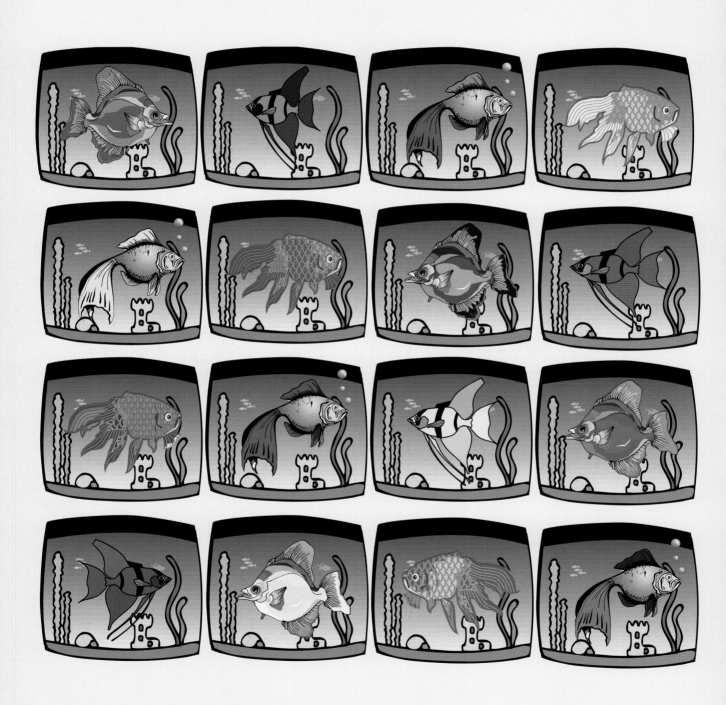

▼ **SYMMETRY LINES (page 94)**

Two patterns do not have eight lines of symmetry (as shown).

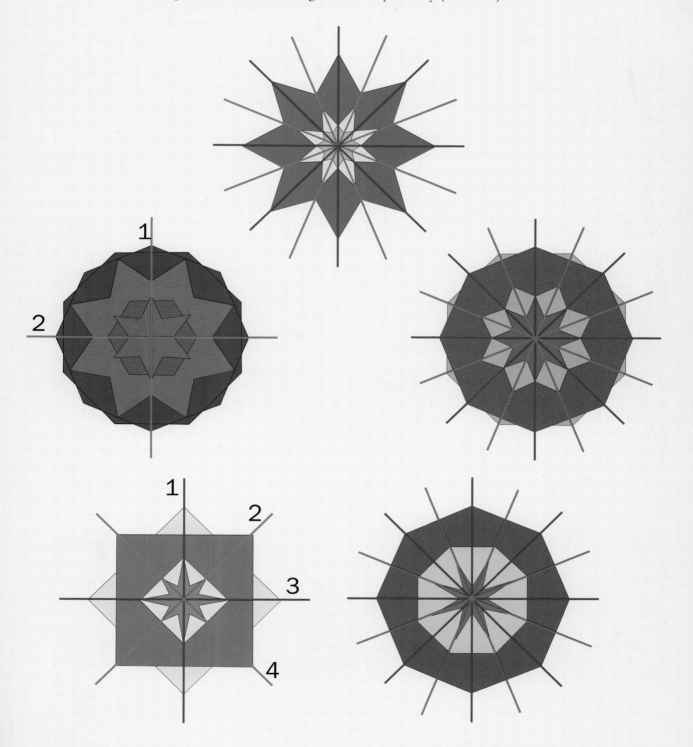

▼ RED DROP (page 95)

In fact, you would see the red drop again, rising from the bowl, exactly 150 milliseconds later. This has been proven using a high-speed camera.

During the short duration of the event, fluid from the red drop does not have enough time to mix with the water in the bowl. This happens every time a tap drips. It is a fantastic demonstration of the complex phenomenon of fluid mechanics known as "reversible laminar flow."

▼ BURNING CANDLE (page 96)

When things burn, they use the oxygen in the air. They cannot burn without it.

When the burning candle has used up all the oxygen in the air, it will go out. The water level in the bottle will rise, taking the place of the used oxygen.

▼ CHEMISTRY EXPERIMENT (page 97)

The six flasks combined can hold a total of 98 units of liquid (two more than a multiple of three).

The empty flask must be one with two more than a multiple of three. The only one to fulfill this requirement is the 20-unit flask.

The remaining five flasks hold 78 units of liquid of which one-third has to be filled with 26 units of red liquid, and the rest with 52 units of blue liquid, as shown.